Post-
Trauma
Stress

Post-Trauma Stress

A personal guide to reduce the long-term effects and hidden emotional damage caused by violence and disaster

— FRANK PARKINSON —

Da Capo

LIFE
LONG

A Member of the Perseus Books Group

Library of Congress
Cataloging-in-Publication Data

Parkinson, Frank.
  Post-trauma stress : a personal guide to reduce the long-term effects and hidden
    emotional damage caused by violence and disaster / Frank Parkinson.
      p. cm.
  Reprint. Previously published in 1993.
  Includes bibliographical references
    and index.
  ISBN-10: 1-55561-249-0   ISBN-13: 978-1-55561-249-8
  1. Post-traumatic stress disorder—Prevention. 2. Psychological debriefing. 3. Loss
  (Psychology)
    I. Title.

RC552.P67 P37 2000
616.85'21—dc21   00-020658

Cover Design: B. Josh Young
Book Design: Randy Schultz

DaCapo Press is a member of the Perseus Books Group
Find us on the World Wide Web at http://www.dacapopress.com

DaCapo Press books are available at special discounts for bulk purchases in the
United States by corporations, institutions, and other organizations. For more
information please contact the Special Markets Department at the Perseus Books
Group, 11 Cambridge Center, Cambridge, MA 02142 or e-mail
special.markets@perseusbooks.com.

Contents

Preface

No man can hide from his own fears,
for they are part of him and they will always know where he is hiding.

—Anonymous

ALL OF US EXPERIENCE STRESS, from the moment we are conceived until the day we die. Stress is an essential and normal part of our daily lives. It enables us to face the problems of life, problems that sometimes produce more stress and that disrupt the peace and calm we seek in what seems to become a more and more hectic world. Stress can be pleasurable when we are riding a roller coaster, watching an exciting movie or cheering our team to win. Dealing with danger and fear in our personal lives, or the lives of those close to us, however, can produce the "fight or flight" response. In this case, stress enables us either to run away or to stay and face the problem.

In many situations in life, the stress generated becomes "di-stress" and we may find it difficult to cope. It may be the result of a bereavement, divorce, moving to a new home, being laid off or fired or some other incident involving change and loss. This stress can be experienced as post-trauma stress, because the feelings generated at the time of the incident have not gone away, but instead have become more difficult and distressing.

Most people will cope, but some suffer various disturbing symptoms. Their suffering is not for a short period, but sometimes for the rest of their lives. Our coping mechanisms work more successfully for some than for others. However, it must be emphasized that post-traumatic stress reactions are *not* abnormal or signs of weakness or inadequacy; they are normal responses to abnormal events. Some will react and others will not, but both responses are normal.

This book is the result of my having been involved over a number of years with people who have experienced incidents such as accidents, disasters, shootings, bombings, armed robberies, hostage situations, riots, war and other trauma-inducing events.

Post-traumatic stress reactions ... are normal responses to abnormal events.

The people I worked with have been from the armed forces, the police, prison, fire-and-rescue and other services, as well as the victims and their families. Many methods of helping and coping exist, but the main emphasis of this book is to share strategies for coping that are already used in other loss situations. In particular I emphasize the model and method used after traumatic incidents known as *psychological debriefing* or *critical incident stress debriefing*. This method has been produced by Atle Dyregrov from Norway, following work done by J. T. Mitchell from the United States and others. This method has been used successfully after a number of different incidents. This kind of debriefing should become standard procedure for all organizations and people who experience traumatic events, whether they recognize that they are suffering or not. The relatively simple procedure needs to be carried out by trained personnel; it will relieve the stress and help to prevent the emergence of the deeper and more disturbing symptoms of post-traumatic stress disorder.

Psychological debriefing should become standard procedure for all organizations and people who experience traumatic events.

I believe we all need to be aware of the effects of difficult and traumatic incidents on our lives and on the lives of those around us. Professionally trained counselors and helpers should be aware of, and can learn, the debriefing method. However, I do not recommend that people use this method who are not properly trained to do so and who do not meet the criteria outlined later in this book.

I hope this material will create further interest in the problems of post-trauma stress and in ways of helping ourselves and others to cope. Stress is always with us, and usually we cope adequately. But when we meet a traumatic incident that is outside the range of our normal experiences, our reactions can be especially painful and deeply disturbing.

Even if our reactions are not painful or disturbing and we feel that we can cope, talking through the experience in a structured way with a trained debriefer can be helpful and encouraging for us, our families and for others involved.

I would like to thank Michael Srinivasan, a psychiatrist, Iris Throp, a social worker, and all those members of the multidisciplinary team who worked together before and after the Gulf War, for their help, encouragement and friendship. I dedicate this book to them and to the converted, and hope for many more in the future! I also give my thanks to Janet Johnston of the Dover Counseling Service, without whom I would not have been introduced to the work of Dyregrov and Mitchell.

Finally, where specific cases are mentioned, these are based on real people and incidents, but in order to protect the identities of those concerned, names and some other details have been changed.

—Frank Parkinson

Introduction

I N RECENT YEARS we have witnessed many disasters worldwide, such as Desert Storm, the United Nations involvement in Bosnia and Serbia, the airline crash of Egypt Air off of the Atlantic seaboard, and various hostage situations. All have brought into focus the devastating effects the events have had on the lives of many of those involved directly and peripherally. Some have died, and their relatives and friends have suffered the terrible pain and loss of bereavement. Others have been injured or maimed physically and will never be the same again. But there are other injuries, not physical, that are much more difficult to identify or understand. A broken leg can be painful and incapacitating, but usually it heals. A shattering emotional experience, however, can cause problems that may include

- Damaged health

- A breakdown of relationships

- A lowered capacity and ability to cope with all areas of life, including marriage and work

It seems obvious that those at the center of an accident or disaster, the victims and survivors, will suffer as a consequence of their experience. Perhaps less obvious are the possible effects of the disaster on the rescuers and helpers. Like ripples on a pond when a stone is thrown into the water, the effects of a traumatic event spread out from the center to include families and friends and many others in an ever-widening circle.

The very real problems caused by the event may be hidden away for many years, only to emerge later with even more disturbing effects.

The stresses and reactions produced by traumatic incidents are similar to those of bereavement and grief. Experiencing a traumatic incident means loss, and loss is an inevitable consequence of human life, from birth to death. Loss brings change and change can mean growth, but growth is often painful and disturbing.

Yet the very pain of loss contains within it the seeds of healing and renewal. Therefore, those who suffer should be aware that what they are experiencing are normal reactions to abnormal events. The way to renew and heal is to move through the pain and not deny its existence. To pretend that the pain does not exist or will simply go away can lead to much deeper and more complicated problems later.

Those who suffer—or who are likely to be involved as carers and helpers of those who suffer—need information, help and support. This book provides information about the process and nature of traumatic reactions and its connection to loss, and describes a way of providing support.

In recent years, our understanding of the nature and process of grief and the effects of being involved in traumatic incidents has grown. Today we are better able than ever before to help others and ourselves to cope after the fact. Studies of the effects of

The debriefing process lets people talk through their experiences in a structured and disciplined way.

disasters and accidents have led to the development of the procedure known as *psychological debriefing* or *critical incident debriefing*. The debriefing process is carried out by trained personnel, usually two or three days after the event, with people who have been in traumatic incidents. This procedure has been shown to lower the possibility of deeper problems emerging at a later stage.

The main focus of the debriefing is to acknowledge that the reactions people are experiencing in connection to the trauma, whatever they are, are normal. The basis of the debriefing is to convey that those involved are *normal people* who have experienced an *abnormal event*. They are *not* mentally or emotionally sick or ill; they are experiencing the normal symptoms of trauma and loss.

The debriefing process lets people talk through their experiences in a structured and disciplined way. They are encouraged to move naturally from the facts as they perceive them to their feelings before and during the event. Next they look at how they feel now, at what they might need and what resources are available to help them in the future. Some may seek psychiatric or counseling help, but most will be able to cope. Debriefing is for everyone and anyone involved in the trauma, from victims and survivors to helpers, carers and, in some instances, entire families. The debriefing method and model is described in detail in chapter 7.

> *Debriefing is for everyone and anyone involved in the trauma.*

Although I was unaware of it at the time, my first involvement in post-trauma stress goes back to 1962, when I was a minister. I bought gasoline at the same station every week. One day the man who was filling my gas tank rested one foot on the car bumper. I noticed an angry, red scar around his lower leg. When I asked about it, he told me that he had been a prisoner of war in Asia and had been chained to a wall for long periods of time, hence the mark on his leg. Whenever I stopped for gas after that he would talk at great length about his experiences. In retrospect I believe he needed to talk, and this helped him come to terms with the experience. There was no such thing as psychological debriefing at mid-century, and he was offered no counseling or help after the war.

After I joined the army, I was asked to help with a number of training courses on general topics such as the social services, basic listening skills and bereavement. At that time I saw the need for changes in attitudes toward all social and health problems, including bereavement and loss, and for more training and cooperation between support agencies and military personnel.

My interest in bereavement and loss had grown when I was based in Germany and had to help people to cope with the deaths of babies and young children. The attitudes of many professional helpers and of some in positions of authority appalled me. I was led by one particular experience of a stillbirth to look at this problem further.

All the familiar attitudes were there: "You'll get over it soon," "Put it behind you and have another baby," "Look to the future," or "It's just one of those things that happen." Even some hospital staff and clergy were content to allow a stillbirth to pass without any kind of formal recognition, without comment; without ritual or burial, without allowing or encouraging the parents to grieve.

These experiences made me even more interested in the processes of loss and grief. I became aware, especially through the media, that others were concerned about this also.

Later I trained as a marriage counselor, and this was one of the most important and influential experiences of my life. It enabled me to look not only at myself, but also at the whole field of counseling and helping. I was able to extend this knowledge and skill into many areas of life.

As a follow-up to a major airplane disaster on a highway, I was asked to speak to military personnel who had helped at the scene. I knew little about post-trauma stress, but knew something about bereavement, loss and counseling. I had also been involved on a number of occasions with soldiers and their families after active duty in a war zone. Because of this I was able to conduct a kind of mini-debriefing, although I knew nothing of Alte Dyregrov and J.T. Mitchell at the time.

My aim was to get those involved to talk.

My aim was to get those involved to talk by giving a presentation on loss and stress, to reassure them that their reactions were normal and that they were not weak or inadequate if they experienced unusual reactions. Many of the women found it easy to talk, but the men generally felt unable to do so. How I wish I had known about psychological debriefing then!

Then I was asked to help a team of prison chaplains after some serious prison riots. I contacted Janet Johnston from the Dover Counseling Center to ask her advice. She asked about my professional training and experiences and then offered to send me information about a helping method called *psychological debriefing*. She encouraged me to look at the material and assured me that it would help. This was my introduction to the work of Atle Dyregrov and J.T. Mitchell. I spent two days with the chaplain team in a retreat and used the model she had sent me. It was such a moving and stimulating experience that I wrote to Dyregrov. He was kind enough to show an interest in my work and encouraged me to use and adapt his model.

After the invasion of Kuwait, before the Gulf War broke out, I visited the military helpline set up in London for the families and relatives of those held hostage in Kuwait and Iraq. I suggested that on their return they would need psychological debriefing. Somewhat to my surprise, this suggestion was adopted by the British Ministry of Defense. Psychological debriefing was provided first for the women who returned and later for the men. Some young adults and children were also involved. This is discussed in more detail later in this chapter.

With these experiences I became even more convinced that those who experience trauma need much more than what is now called *defusing*—help and encouragement at the time of the incident and shortly after. Psychological debriefing helps them come to terms with their experiences and lessens the possibility of deeper psychological problems emerging later.

At the same time, a group of soldiers was being trained for the British Army Graves Registration Team for the Gulf War with the expectation that there could be large numbers of casualties. When asked if I would help, I spent a morning with these men and encouraged them to look at all their anxieties and worries. I was surprised that when asked to discuss this topic in small groups, they were able to produce an almost textbook set of responses. It was all there: concern for their families at home; fear of dying and of combat, the desire to do the best for the dead and their relatives.

Would they be able to cope? What about the macho image they were supposed to show? Would they be able to deal with the dead bodies? How would they react? Would it become easier or more difficult? How would they cope if they knew the dead? Would they make mistakes? Would they cope with the heat and periods of boredom? Would they be able to sleep and rest? How would the experience affect them when they returned home? What would be the effects on their families? Theirs would be a difficult and distressing task, and they knew it. On their return from the Gulf and at the request of their commanding officer, these soldiers participated in psychological debriefing overseen by members of the team who had debriefed the Gulf hostages.

How would the experience affect them when they returned home? What would be the effects on their families?

Because of this involvement and experience, I was asked to help people after car accidents and other traumatic incidents. This spread into the civilian world, and the local police invited me to help people who were suffering trauma after various incidents, including a fatal shooting and a violent family-hostage situation. Little help was available except to refer victims to a psychiatrist, clinical psychologist or counselor. Many of these professionals knew very little about the problems of post-trauma stress or of the method of helping through psychological debriefing.

During my next assignments, I worked with employees following bank and armed robberies, and with some survivors of terrorist bombings. More recently I was asked to evaluate the problem of stress for social-work personnel.

Perhaps not surprisingly, I found that most people just wanted to talk, but also I found that the strategies they used for coping with the stress of their work were identical to those used by helpers in disaster situations. It seems that trauma produces similar coping mechanisms in people, whatever the situation.

It seems that trauma produces similar coping mechanisms in people, whatever the situation.

All of these experiences convinced me that normal counseling is not sufficient to help those who suffer from post-trauma stress. The process of psychological debriefing should be an essential element in our response to victims and helpers after traumatic incidents. All that is needed is knowledge of post-trauma stress and its effects and influences on those involved and a group of counselors trained in the Dyregrov and Mitchell method and model. Psychological debriefing could and should be written into the standard response of organizations and

[My] experiences convinced me that normal counseling is not sufficient to help those who suffer from post-trauma stress.

institutions such as the armed forces, police, fire and rescue services, banks, hospitals and medical services.

It seems simple to do, but this is not the case, because there is a basic resistance in many people and organizations to any kind of helping response other than defusing and counseling. Counseling can help, but psychological debriefing is far more effective and the benefit is enormous.

When the invasion of Kuwait occurred in 1990, a large number of individuals and families from the United Kingdom and other countries were held hostage. At that time, some members of a closely knit team of more than 80 families based in Kuwait were on vacations away from the Gulf. They immediately set up a help line in London for relatives and families back home. These helpers experienced feelings of guilt and regret that they were not with their friends when the crisis broke out. They felt much anxiety and concern, not only about their friends in Kuwait and Iraq, but also for their own homes there.

They had left irreplaceable personal belongings behind, and their lives were focused on their friends and colleagues in the Gulf. They had lost their homes, places of work, their community and also personal possessions, some of which were of deep sentimental value.

One man expressed this simply when he said that it felt awful to think that strangers were looking at photographs of his daughter. There was also great concern for their Kuwaiti friends and neighbors. Running this network provided an essential service for the relatives of the families at home but it also met a deep need for those who were running the help line. They felt useful and needed, were kept informed about whatever was happening and were in constant touch with anxious and worried relatives of the hostages.

At a later stage, most of the wives and children were allowed to return home, although a few opted to stay with their husbands. A multidisciplinary team was created to carry out psychological debriefing on their return. This team consisted of chaplains, social workers, hospital social-services personnel, two psychiatrists and a clinical psychologist, all of whom had extensive experience in counseling and group work. They met and trained together and then performed debriefing when the hostages returned. Those who had been running the help line were included.

Some hostages coped afterward by keeping in touch, especially by telephone. . . . Some experienced a sense of intense isolation, and they did not want to be in contact with others, even with those who were close friends.

Some hostages coped afterward by keeping in touch, especially by telephone. They contacted each other regularly and provided a wide network of support and information. Most attended the voluntary debriefings which also included sessions giving advice and help about housing, finance and insurance.

However, not everybody felt able to take part. Some experienced a sense of intense isolation, and they did not want to be in contact with others, even with those who were close friends. A few were unable to do things such as filling out forms or making even simple decisions. And, because of their feelings of anger, disorientation, confusion, loneliness and the separation from their husbands, a few thought they were going crazy. Some also felt a strong resistance to the debriefing process and said that they didn't want to be counseled. This was partly the result of the powerful defense of denial, which will be discussed later.

The fact that debriefing was not counseling was irrelevant. They felt vulnerable and threatened. This was the first time that debriefing had been carried out under such circumstances in the army. Debriefing was not seen as part of the normal response to crisis and some thought it was only for those who acknowledged that they were suffering or who showed signs of distress.

Part of my thesis in this book is that debriefing should not be optional. It is not a luxury for a select few or for those who are overtly in need. It is for *all* those involved, victims and helpers alike, and should be *standard procedure* whenever there is a crisis or traumatic incident. This was expressed by some of the hostages when they were offered psychological debriefing:

> When we landed, we expected a physical and a normal debriefing, but we also needed someone to talk to about what we had been through and how we felt. We got the first two, but not the third, until now.

Those involved had many different reactions. Among the wives who returned early, impulsive actions were not unusual.

> June's husband was a hostage, and she said that when he was released and came home she would meet him at the airport. She would rent an expensive car—perhaps a Porsche or Maserati—and park it outside the airport. When her husband stepped off the plane she would hug and kiss him and then take him outside and say, "There you are, love, I've sold the house and spent all our money on a car for you." She said she was joking, but there was an element of truth behind it.
>
> She too was going through trauma and loss and had a strong desire to do something extravagant for her husband when he returned. It was an impulsive statement, which expressed her elation at the prospect of her ordeal and that of her husband coming to an end. But it also said a great deal about her anxiety, fear and sense of loss. Fortunately, she didn't carry out her threat. I dread to think of her husband's reaction if she had done it!

Many wives had strong feelings of guilt and extreme anger during the hostage situation. They blamed themselves and everyone else they could think of because the situation had been allowed to happen in the first place and because they had left their husbands behind. The uncertainty about the outcome in the Gulf added another element of fear; underneath all the feelings for the wives was the possibility that they might never see their husbands again. Fortunately this did not happen and eventually these men were allowed to come home, just before the war broke out.

Some lose their faith completely and others find it.

Similarly, some soldiers left behind by units who went to the Gulf felt guilty and frustrated that they were not with their friends, even though they knew they were performing an essential task in caring for the families of those who had gone. Some wanted to be with the activated unit because this was where they felt a sense of belonging and comradeship. In addition to this, if some of their friends were killed, they would feel even more guilty about having stayed behind. In this situation, anger, frustration, blame and guilt were all typical symptoms.

Such feelings are not confined to hostage situations or war. Riots can produce powerful feelings of anger and frustration on the part of those who are there as helpers and carers. A minister involved in a riot received many letters of support from Christian groups throughout the country. They said they were praying for him and thinking about him. During the debriefing after the event, when discussing anger, he said

> I was glad for their support, but some letters made me so
> angry that I could have hit the people who wrote them.
> Many quoted the verse from the New Testament, which
> says that for those who love God everything works for
> good (Romans 8, verse 28). This made me angry in two
> ways. First, because in the midst of the turmoil,
> destruction and fear of the event, I did not feel that it
> was relevant and it didn't help. They didn't understand
> what was happening and how devastated I felt. Second, I
> was angry because for years I have used the same
> quotation myself to others . . .

This minister had come to look at his faith in a new light, and this would influence the way he responded to people in distress.

> The minister visited a house at random and a woman
> came to the door who said, "I won't invite you in
> because I am not a Christian. I was, but I lost my faith
> when I served as a nurse in the Spanish Civil War. I saw
> such terrible things, and if people can treat each other
> like that, there can't be a God."

However, in the same parish there was a man in the church choir who had been a regular member since World War II. He often said that before the war he didn't have a faith, but he saw such inhumanity and suffering during the war that he came to believe there must be something better, and so he found Christianity.

Similar experiences of traumatic events can have very different effects among different people. Some seem to need others while a few feel a sense of isolation and loneliness and want to be left alone. Some lose faith and others find it, and many who experience tragedy and trauma in their lives and the lives of those around them often ask questions about meaning and purpose.

- What's the point and purpose of life?
- Is there any reason to live, and is the world a good place to live?
- Are there such things as justice and truth?
- Is life fair?
- Does God exist and, if so, what is God like?
- Why do awful things happen to people who don't deserve it—or do they?
- Why did this happen to me and my family?
- Why is life like this?

Some come to believe there is no point and no God and that life is not worth living. A few might be so desolate that they lose the will to carry on. The answer for them, if there is one, lies in suicide. There is no point in anything any more and nothing to live for.

Others find faith in atheism or humanism, or reject any kind of orthodox belief. Others turn to religion or seek answers and comfort in spiritualism and mysticism. Some have difficulty in making simple decisions.

> Ted was a policeman who came home in the middle of a
> riot that had lasted a few days and was likely to
> continue. As he walked into the house, his wife spoke to
> him: "Hello, darling. What would you like for dinner,
> steak and potatoes or a hamburger and fries?" Ted
> couldn't cope with this and was unable to decide. Not
> only that, he became very angry and shouted, "What the
> hell does it matter?" He said later that he was going
> through such turmoil in his mind and was surrounded by
> so much violence and hatred that the question struck him
> as trivial beyond words. "I'm going through this," he said,
> "and she asks me that!"

A soldier who returned from the Gulf War said

> I could not settle down. Making simple decisions was
> difficult. Even getting out of bed and making the effort to
> go to work was almost more than I could handle.
> Throughout the day I felt listless and tired and just
> couldn't be bothered with anything or anyone.
> Everything was just too much trouble for me.

Another common response to crisis and disaster is that things that were once very important can become irrelevant.

> If you have a lovely home and your family has been
> killed in a disaster, then your home doesn't seem to
> matter any more. The people who made it a home rather
> than a house have gone. Material things become
> unimportant. After all, they are only things and not
> people. Also, there is no real value or sense in having
> status in life, a job or in achieving and succeeding. What
> good is the house now that you are on your own and
> have lost those you love?

The opposite can happen. Things that were perhaps not very important or were taken for granted, particularly objects, can assume a value seemingly out of proportion to their worth. In particular, buildings can become the focus of people's emotions and feelings. This was true in the Manchester prison riots, in which the prison building was seen by some not just as a place of work, but endowed with almost human characteristics and personality. The prison was a closely knit community of people, like a walled town.

Atle Dyregrov wrote a letter about this:

> I was struck by the phenomenon that you mention, and that I have noticed in several of the disasters that I have worked with; namely, how material objects can have a very strong symbolic value. I remember vividly from my work with the California earthquake in 1989 how the inhabitants of Santa Cruz described the enormous emotional effect it had on them that the [pedestrian] mall had been destroyed.

This mall represented the heart of the city, and its destruction affected the lives of many in the community. With disaster workers, it is often not the destruction and mutilation of a human body that strikes them hardest, but seeing a child's toy or some other symbolic object that brings the personal ramifications of the event closer.

People identify very strongly with their place of work. Closing down an industry or business is a disaster that brings a deep sense of personal loss for those involved.

Those who lose their homes in a disaster can have similar responses. Buildings, toys, shoes and other objects can be the focus of our emotions because they remind us what the event has cost in terms of human and personal suffering. Perhaps the closest to this in other areas is the importance of a ship to the crew who see it not just as an object, but refer to it as "she," as though it were human. Its loss and sinking can have a devastating effect upon them.

A regiment in the army, its flag or standard and its tradition, can have a similar personal identity, and some will mourn the loss of their battalion, regiment or corps in a war or in any changes that take place through military restructuring. Breaking this powerful sense of attachment to objects or closely knit groups can evoke very strong feelings of loss.

This can also apply in cases where communities rely on a factory, coal mine, shipyard, store or other industry for their welfare. People identify very strongly with their place of work. Closing down an industry or business is a disaster that brings a deep sense of personal loss for those involved. Bricks and mortar become humanized and identified as the focus for feelings of acute and painful loss. This extends to the experiences of layoffs and unemployment, which can also result in trauma and feelings of rejection and loss.

Some or all of these symptoms can be experienced in what might be seen as minor events when compared with major disasters. Car accidents, accidents at work, having an operation, being fired or laid off, dealing with a divorce or separation, moving to a different house, being involved in violence, witnessing a traumatic incident can all trigger problems. They can result in feelings of guilt and anger, isolation and loneliness, vulnerability and depression, loss of faith and self-worth, changes in values and attitudes, fear and shame, nightmares and sleep disturbances, marital breakdown and illness, self-blame and bitterness. All of these are symptoms of loss and trauma.

Basic Beliefs

The loss experience disrupts the basic beliefs and feelings we have grown to accept throughout our lives so that they have become part of our agenda and expectation. It is as though we have a huge pack on our backs, which gradually is being filled with experiences as we grow and develop. When we face any situation, we reach into the pack for the tools we need in order to cope.

Some of these tools are the beliefs we have absorbed, and we build ourselves and the pattern of our lives around them until they are disturbed, or we find they don't seem to fit the situation or our needs. There are three basic beliefs that we all accept in some measure and have put into our packs as tools.

Invulnerability

We tend to think that life is fairly safe and secure: "Bad things happen to other people and not to me." Our general experience of life is that most of us do survive without being involved in major accidents or disasters. Our very strong defense mechanisms are there to protect us from becoming overanxious. We live our lives as optimists, in the false belief that we will live forever and that harm or danger will not touch us.

When we are suddenly confronted by a traumatic and shattering experience, our safe little world can collapse or be turned upside down, resulting in confusion and fear.

- "Your wife has left you for another man."

- "I'm sorry, your husband has had a heart attack at work."

- "You have cancer and six months to live."

Other experiences can have similar effects, such as being a survivor in a car crash, accident or disaster, being raped, violently assaulted or held hostage, witnessing or being involved in violence, war, murder, suicide, shootings or robberies. Experiencing any of these events make us aware that we are not invulnerable. We are mortal. We can die. Life is neither secure nor safe. It is uncertain and sometimes appears to be the result of malevolent and impersonal forces. These experiences can cause intense fear and anxiety, as well as the loss of security and confidence in yourself, others or life in general.

Meaning and purpose

Most of the time we feel that we have a reason to live. Meaning and purpose can come from happy and satisfying relationships, a good job, achieving success and from the firm belief that life makes sense. It might come from religious belief. Incidents and experiences that induce trauma and stress call this basic belief into question.

If your child is killed or dies, then your life has been devastated. Similarly, if you are involved in an accident or disaster, your world can be shattered. There isn't meaning or purpose in what happened. Life loses meaning when such tragedies occur and any purpose you thought there was in living is questioned.

Similarly, if you are involved in war and conflict, where you see death and destruction close at hand, or your life is threatened and you think you are going to die, then you can wonder what all this is for and if there is any sense or reason behind it. This can cause intense and overwhelming fear, anger and frustration, and the desire to scream at the universe about the injustice of life.

The result of these disturbances can be the loss of any sense of purpose in living. It can lead to the conclusion that life is without meaning, a sick joke and an utter waste of time. In some cases drawing this conclusion can result in depression, a sense of pointlessness and even suicide.

Self-respect

Most people have a reasonably positive image of themselves and believe that they are fairly good and decent citizens who would, in difficult circumstances, do whatever they could to help others. Therefore we can build up a strong image of ourselves where we have developed a sense of self-worth and self-esteem.

Difficult experiences can harm or destroy our personal images of self-worth and self-esteem.

Difficult experiences can harm or destroy these images. Those involved in an accident where others are killed or injured can feel that they might have acted differently. "Perhaps I could have saved somebody's life," or "If only I'd left home ten minutes later, then this would not have happened."

We can lose our sense of dignity and worth and feel guilt, anger, regret, resentment and bitterness. The foundations of our world begin to crumble and the ground begins to shake under our feet. We begin to question our own self-worth and value as a human being. The symptoms that can follow the destruction or questioning of the basic foundations of our life beliefs are similar to those of bereavement and grief.

We are shocked. We feel a great sense of anger. We become depressed and lose the belief that we can go on. These feelings may be compounded by others: loss of reality, numbness, guilt and blame, regret and rejection, helplessness and loss of purpose, isolation and loneliness, loss of identity and meaning. Given time, most of us will be able to work through the pain and come to healing. With patience, help and understanding we can rediscover a sense of purpose in our lives and slowly renew our feelings of self-worth.

The problem is that it can be a long and painful process and, because of this, it is necessary for both victims and helpers to be aware of the nature and symptoms of post-trauma stress so they know what is happening to them and why. Also, they need to know what can be done to help them. In this chapter, I have suggested some typical effects trauma and stress have on people. I'll go on to examine the symptoms in more detail so we can understand how widely they can affect people and what can happen to those involved.

We will look at loss as a common experience in human life and its connection with traumatic reactions. We will also examine the involvement and experiences of helpers. Last, we consider the method and model of psychological debriefing as a normal response to those involved in trauma and how it can help them understand their experiences and cope better with their lives.

2

What Is Post-Trauma Stress?

ANY INCIDENT WE EXPERIENCE that is sudden and unexpected can result in emotional as well as physical trauma and shock. This emotional shock can cause stress reactions, which are called *post-trauma stress* or *critical incident stress.* This kind of stress therefore results from experiencing a traumatic incident and can be the result of anything from a slight accident to involvement in a major disaster.

> Billy, age 4, has fallen off his bicycle and runs to his mother, crying. He has bruised both knees as well as his pride. His mother puts her arms around him, comforts him and asks what happened. He sobs out his story. He was riding down the path on his new bike when suddenly the front wheel slipped and he crashed onto the ground. He has hurt his knee and his bike is still lying where it fell. He is sobbing gently in his mother's arms, breathing in short gasps.
>
> He tells her that it's a rotten bike anyway, and it was the bike's fault, and he's never going to ride it again, ever! His mother holds him and tells him that he'll be all right. She will go with him to get his bike and bring it home, and then he can ride it again when he feels better. She puts ointment on his knee and some tender loving care on his pride and gradually he stops crying. She takes his hand and both go outside and get the bike. He is frightened at first, but with her beside him holding the seat, he climbs onto it again and slowly pedals down the pathway, wobbling from side to side.

A simple incident, but one that represents a major step in Billy's life. He is shocked and crying, runs to his mother for help and comfort, tells his story and she helps him regain the confidence to ride his bicycle again. He is suffering from physical pain and from the mental and emotional shock and stress caused by the unexpected fall. If his mother had told him not to be stupid and had not offered him comfort, but had forced him to "get out there and be a man," either he would have been afraid of bikes for the rest of his life or gritted his teeth and climbed back on again.

However, his mother might have taken a different approach: "Don't worry about that nasty little bike. Just leave it there in the road, and when Daddy comes home, he'll get rid of it. Tomorrow we'll get you a nice football. That can't hurt you."

Billy's reaction to any of these responses from his mother could have been very different. He might have buried his fears, had dreams or nightmares about the fall, kept away from bicycles forever and cried or screamed with fear whenever one came near. Equally likely, he could cope by forcing himself to conquer his fear, but this fear could have emerged in some other way, either at the time or later.

This is an exaggerated example, but note that even a relatively simple incident can cause reactions of stress and trauma. Billy has experienced some of the typical symptoms of post-trauma stress—shock, pain, fear, crying, blaming, avoidance and the need for help and comfort. A traumatic incident can be far more serious than falling off a bicycle.

> *Billy has experienced some of the typical symptoms of post-trauma stress—shock, pain, fear, crying, blaming, avoidance and the need for help and comfort.*

> Andy was driving his car very carefully down the highway at a steady 60 miles per hour. It was almost midnight and he was on his way home from a party at a friend's house 50 miles away. Jim, his best friend, was in the front passenger seat asleep. Andy knew that Jim was excited because he was meeting his girlfriend the next day. She was at college and he had not seen her for four weeks. It was slightly foggy, and Andy was driving with great care.

Suddenly he saw a bright light flash into his eyes and there was a loud bang. The next thing he knew, the car was spinning around. There was a second loud noise and the car stopped with a crash. He was dazed for a few seconds, but managed to open the door of the car and stagger out. He felt he had to get away from the danger. There was blood on his face and his left arm was hanging by his side.

He saw a car behind him and the driver came forward and asked if he could help. They looked into the car and found that Jim was obviously dead. Within minutes, the police and an ambulance arrived and Andy was taken to a hospital where he was found to be suffering from a broken arm, concussion and severe cuts and bruises to the head. Because he was also suffering from shock, he was kept in the hospital for more than a week and then sent home. He was back at work in the factory within two weeks.

His boss found that Andy was acting rather strangely. Andy couldn't concentrate and sometimes just stared vacantly into space. He talked about not sleeping and when he did he had nightmares. He even thought he saw Jim looking at him through a window in the factory office and in the rear-view mirror of his car. His boss told him to go home and see his doctor. While he was in the hospital Andy had been visited regularly by a doctor and the chaplain. They both told him that it had been a terrible accident, but he must remember that he was not to blame. A man had been driving on the wrong side of the highway and had hit his car almost head-on.

Jim had been killed because he was not wearing his seat belt. Andy had known about the seat belt, but had not said anything at the time because Jim was relaxed and asleep. In the hospital, Andy was very distressed, not only because of the shock, but because of Jim's death and because he had not been able to attend the funeral. The doctor told him that he would be all right and that although it was a tragedy he should put it behind him and remember that it wasn't his fault. Other staff members told him the same thing. More than a month later he went to his doctor. Unfortunately the doctor didn't know much about this kind of condition and gave him antidepressants.

Many doctors, hospital staff, clergy, social workers, counselors and other helpers do not understand post-trauma stress. And there is sometimes the belief, as with bereavement, that people will "soon get over it" and be back to normal within a relatively short time. There is still a common attitude that such experiences, no matter how traumatic and difficult, can be dealt with simply by not letting them get you down. "Keep a stiff upper lip and get on with life," or, "When the going gets tough, the tough get going." The attitude is that all you need to do is put it out of your mind and just get on with your life.

Many doctors, hospital staff, clergy, social workers, counselors and other helpers do not understand post-trauma stress.

We have either forgotten or do not know that when we experience something that is horrifying, intensely disturbing, or shocking and painful, it does not go away. It becomes part of our experience and can result in disturbing and frightening symptoms, especially if we do not acknowledge our initial feelings and deny their existence. The feelings and emotions become buried in our minds and lie there, slowly affecting everyone around them—waiting for the opportunity to emerge and influence other areas of our lives.

Most of us are not tough enough to face the disasters and losses that come to us because we have never faced them or experienced them before. The resulting symptoms can be extremely disturbing, even disabling, and might destroy our lives so that we cannot cope, our families and friends cannot cope with us, our marriages break down, we are unable to work. Our health begins to suffer. Only in recent years have we begun to study and understand the symptoms we now call *post-trauma stress,* although they have been identified and known for many years under different names.

Shell Shock

During World War I doctors identified a condition known generally as *shell shock* because it was believed to be induced by the explosion of shells on the battlefield. The symptoms were numerous and disturbing. They included twitching and shaking of limbs, catatonic states, inability to sleep or relax, manic behavior, depression, loss of speech and memory, and even paralysis.

> A story I remember from the 1950s told of an officer in World War I who suffered from paralysis of his right hand and was taken out of the front line. At that point his condition improved. Every time he went back into the line, the condition appeared again. The explanation given was that when troops went "over the top," they were led by an officer who normally carried a pistol in his right hand.
>
> This man's fear was so great that he repressed it, but it surfaced as a psychosomatic reaction in which his right hand was immobilized. If he couldn't use his right hand, then he couldn't go with his men into battle. He was dealing with his fear by pushing it down into his mind, but he could not prevent it from emerging as a physical symptom, even though he was unaware of its cause.

Though this may have been a fictional story, it contains seeds of truth about the probable causes of the condition known as *shell shock*—intense fear, the desire to run away and escape, the belief that this was not the right thing to do, the sights and sounds of the battlefield, plus the horror and experience, or imminence, of battle.

Some men who were shot as deserters or labeled as cowards are now believed to have been suffering from post-trauma stress. Many deserters did not show physical signs of illness except that they were extremely frightened and had run away. Some who suffered symptoms of stress did receive understanding and treatment, but it seems that in such circumstances as the terror and carnage of World War I, there was little sympathy for those who showed a cowardly streak.

Almost every home in Britain and many in the United States were affected by this war. The sheer numbers of casualties were unimaginable. On the first day of the Battle of the Somme, 60,000 men were killed or injured. Little wonder that those who were unable to cope were often despised, treated as deserters and, on some occasions, executed. There were, however, some who were more enlightened. One chaplain writing home from the front said

> No words can tell you how I feel, nor can words tell you
> of the horrors of the clearing of a battlefield. This
> battalion was left to do just that and several men went
> off with shell shock and two more were wounded. I am
> certain the shell shock was caused not just by the
> explosion of shells nearby, but by the sight, smell and
> horror of the battlefield in general. I felt dreadful.

He believed that this condition was due to the sheer horror induced by the total experience of being on the battlefield—the fear and terror, the noise of explosions and the screams of men, the smells and sights, the carnage, the bodies, the mud and blood and the death and destruction of war. For him, these were the true causes of shell shock.

Combat Fatigue

Eventually shell shock became known as *battle shock, battle fatigue, combat fatigue* or *battle stress,* and was recognized as a specific reaction to war and conflict. In World War II, when possible, troops were given periods of rest and even leave. Some aircrews were allowed to fly only a certain number of missions before they were relieved of duty. Today, soldiers serving on short tours of duty are given "R & R," rest and recreation, in the middle of their tour of duty. This recognizes that they need a break, that they need to see their families and their families need to see them. It is intended to reduce the strain and stress for all concerned and to lessen the likelihood of problems arising.

The experiences of soldiers who served during the Vietnam War served as a major step forward in our understanding of what can happen to men on the battlefield and afterward. In preparing the soldiers for combat, training sessions were included on the possible psychological effects of war and combat. Some claim this significantly reduced the number of psychological casualties.

However, when the men returned home there was a general reluctance to accept them or to see them as heroes fighting in a just war, and this compounded their problems.

Some soldiers responded with feelings of intense anger and frustration and suffered the trauma of mental breakdown. Some were unable to take or keep a job, while others could not make or keep stable relationships and their marriages broke down. There were feelings of anger, bitterness and guilt, and some blamed themselves for what had happened. Some dropped out of "normal" society and formed communes or lived in isolation. Others could see no point in living and committed suicide. There were emotional and psychological casualties from earlier wars also, where the symptoms were not quite so obvious.

> Dennis had been a soldier in World War II, and this seemed to be the high point of his life. He could talk about nothing else. If you said, "What a lovely day. Just look at the sun shining on those trees," he would say, "Yes, I remember it was just like that when we were outside Paris. It was a Thursday—no, it was Tuesday, because that German Messerschmitt came over, and we were in this orchard and my buddy had caught some chickens and we were going to have them for dinner.
>
> "And this officer came over and told us to go down to the crossroads to see if it was clear, and when we got there we saw some soldiers on the other side of this gully, and I said that they were our soldiers. But my buddy said they didn't look like them and then we saw they were Germans, so we ran back to the camp and thought that we weren't going to be dead heroes.
>
> "And when we got back we saw this cow in a field and decided to have steak for supper and there was this ruined house and . . ."

He never fails to tell a long and complicated story, no matter what is said to him—so people avoid talking to him. He finds difficulty in facing the world of today and continually lives in the past.

If Dennis felt able to talk about the more difficult and disturbing things he experienced, he might find that he could begin to come to terms with his feelings.

Part of the problem for Dennis is that he talks constantly about things that are either humorous or general —never about any disturbing events such as the death of friends or his experience of battle. If Dennis felt able to talk about the more difficult and disturbing things he experienced, he might find that he could begin to come to terms with his feelings. Also, he might discover that he has less need to talk and would be able to live more in the present.

Unlike Dennis, some survivors are unable to talk about their experience at all, and they bury what happened to them deep inside, to cover it up. The problem is that their strong feelings about it can emerge many years later.

> Andrew was 66 and a businessman who worked one evening a week as a volunteer helper for a local organization. He was attending a course on bereavement and stress to help with his work. The lecturer was showing a video about the Falklands conflict, in which a young soldier was talking about burying the dead. The lecturer noticed Andrew looking at the floor and thought that he must be bored or uninterested.
>
> After the session, they had a break for coffee. Andrew approached the lecturer and said, "I'm sorry about that. You probably thought I was being rude, but I was a young medic in France during World War II, and my unit was attacked by an enemy fighter. Afterward I had to help pick up and bury what was left of some of my friends. I was terrified at the time and we never talked about it. I had to do this a number of times. I know now that this has been with me for over 45 years, hovering in the back of my mind, and I've never come to terms with it. I need help. I need someone to talk to."

Coping with Combat Stress

Many modern armies have strategies for helping people to cope with battle stress. This method has been called *the 5 Rs,* because it involves Removal, Rest, Recounting, Reassurance and Return.

Removal

Once symptoms are recognized, the soldier is moved to a position not far behind the front line. It is essential not to evacuate him or treat him as someone who is ill or sick. He is not hospitalized or turned into a patient. The emphasis is on the normality of his reactions. He is allowed to keep his uniform, combat kit and weapons, so he remains a soldier on duty and not a patient in pajamas. Where possible, he is kept in touch with his friends and comrades and made aware of what's happening to them.

Rest

The soldier is allowed time to rest and relax to the extent possible, and this is helped by his removal from the noise and confusion of the front. He may also be able to sleep or perform light duties, especially where he is helping others and feels useful.

Recounting

The soldier is encouraged to talk about what has been happening to him and hopefully he is able to speak about his feelings and anxieties. This should be done with someone who takes an uncritical, nonjudgmental attitude toward him. He is seen and treated as a normal soldier temporarily affected by what he has experienced around and within him. Talking helps him to bring out his fears and face them in a supportive environment.

Reassurance

One major fear is that such reactions might suggest to a soldier that he is a coward or a failure, is going crazy or is letting down his friends and unit, or that he is weak or suffering from what was once called IMF (lack of moral fiber!). He is given assurance that he is not weak, feeble or having a nervous breakdown—that his reactions are normal—and that he will soon be back with his unit. Reassurance that his reactions and feelings are normal is essential.

Return

After a relatively short period of time, the soldier should be able to return to duty with his unit and continue as normal. When he returns, he goes back to his usual duties and is expected to continue with his work surrounded by the familiarity, friendship and support of his comrades.

This process could include another R—Recovery—because if the procedure is successful, he will recover fully. The overriding emphasis is placed on treating him as a human being, someone who is experiencing normal reactions to abnormal events; he is not a coward, a wimp or weak.

Similar strategies are used by therapists, counselors and psychiatrists when dealing with certain conditions in individuals or in family therapy. This is mentioned by John Cleese and Robin Skynner in chapter 2 of their book, *Families and How to Survive Them*. Skynner speaks of everyone having an internal "mental map" of his or her world. When something traumatic happens, this map has to be changed and adjusted. He explains that in order to adjust we need

- Rest—time off and space to breathe

- Reassurance—that all will be well

- Emotional support—someone just being there with us

This is similar to the method described above that is used to help soldiers suffering from combat stress or fatigue and it can be applied to all occasions when we are faced with sudden change or trauma.

This method of treating traumatic symptoms gives us a clue about how to define post-trauma stress. It is the reaction experienced from being involved in a traumatic incident, such as a sudden shock, a death in the family, or witnessing an accident or disaster, or an ongoing experience such as a war or being held hostage.

> *Symptoms of post-trauma stress can also be found before the incident is over.*

Symptoms of post-trauma stress can also be found before the incident is over. A soldier on the battlefield is not necessarily suffering from post-trauma stress, but has to endure constant stress, perhaps over a long period of time. He might suffer during the battle, but control his emotions and feelings, or he might develop and show symptoms and receive help.

However, it is afterward, when he moves away from the field of battle, or when the battle is over and he returns home, that he might suffer from post-traumatic stress reactions. Similarly, those involved in accidents or disasters as helpers might find themselves undergoing stress while carrying out their duties and further stress later, after they've left the scene.

These days, an enormous industry surrounds the whole problem of stress in our society. There are relaxation tapes and videos, classes to attend, yoga, meditation techniques, books and pamphlets—all to help people learn to relax and cope with the pressures of modern living. Events of recent years, especially following traumatic incidents, have also brought the problems of coping with stress sharply into focus.

We have seen the Gulf War, the Balkans conflict, and many disasters, such as Hurricanes Andrew and Floyd, South Dakota floods, air and train crashes, fires, bombings and shootings, and the traumas caused by acts of terrorism and murder.

Disasters affect people other than those immediately involved. The return of the hostages from the Middle East has shown how their incarceration affected their families and friends. Terry Waite, Terry Anderson and many others have been seen and interviewed on television and in other media. Their faces alone have spoken volumes about how they were affected by their experiences of isolation and sometimes brutal or violent treatment. These people have endured something beyond our imagination, and they will probably find it difficult to come to terms with their experiences.

They suffered physical and mental stresses that will not go away just because they have returned home.

They suffered physical and mental stresses that will not go away just because they have returned home. They have to adjust to their new freedom and relate to the many changes that have taken place in themselves, in their families and friends and in the world around them. Their stress is of a particular kind in that it was something they experienced over a long period of time. It was not the sharp or sudden shock of an accident or disaster. For some, the reactions have been extremely intense and disturbing, while others appear to have coped quite well, but they will still, to a greater or lesser degree, suffer some of the symptoms typical of post-trauma stress.

Post-Trauma Stress: A Definition

What then is post-trauma stress? At its simplest it can be defined as "the normal reactions of normal people to events that for them are unusual or abnormal." The problem arises as to which events, for us, are unusual or abnormal. For most of us it is not normal to be involved in a disaster or accident or to have our lives threatened; the effects of such incidents on the human mind and body can be quite dramatic and traumatic.

We do not expect to face sudden shock or trauma: the car, airplane or train crash; the hooded gunman shouting or screaming at us; ourselves lying in the gutter, beaten up and robbed by thugs. Even when we are trained to do a difficult job, the effects can still be traumatic. The police marksman or soldier trained to shoot at people, the fireman or doctor, can still be traumatized by what they see and sometimes have to do.

All of these incidents, and many more, can result in some of the symptoms of post-trauma stress. This applies not only to those who are victims or survivors, but also to their families, to those who are called in to help, and even onlookers and witnesses. One method of helping is by using psychological debriefing, also called *critical incident stress debriefing*, which is covered in detail in chapter 8.

Most survivors of trauma will experience post-trauma stress, but in different intensities at the time or later and for different lengths of time after the incident. Some may be slightly distressed for a few hours or a few days and then recover quite naturally and continue with their lives. Others suffer longer, and if the symptoms persist and intensify for more than a month, these people are usually identified as suffering from post-traumatic stress disorder (PTSD). They will need treatment. Post-traumatic stress disorder is defined in the American Psychiatric Association publication *Diagnostic and Statistical Manual of Mental Disorders* (revised 1995), as "The development of certain characteristic symptoms following a psychologically distressing event that is outside the range of normal human experience." Again, the problem is what is and what is not "normal." PTSD is discussed further in chapter 8, and in *Coping with Catastrophe* by Peter Hodgkinson and Michael Stewart.

Not everyone will suffer the symptoms of post-traumatic stress, but remember: It is normal to react, but you can be normal and not react.

In other words, some will show signs of stress reactions and these can be mild or intense, short-lived or long-lasting, while others will seem to be unaffected in any way. The wide variation of responses makes it impossible to tell who is suffering and who is not. It is easy to look at survivors and assume that because A is screaming, shouting and running around while B is calm and cool, that A is suffering and B is not. However, A might be coping better than B because he or she is letting his or her emotions and feelings emerge. B might be bottling up everything inside and defending himself or herself against reacting.

> *It is said that the three most traumatic events we can experience, in descending order, are: bereavement, divorce and moving to another house. All of these can result in stress and post-trauma stress.*

This can be like trying to keep the cork on a fizzing bottle of champagne. Sooner or later the champagne explodes and blows the cork high into the air. Human emotions can be the same. I might hold my feelings inside and then suddenly "blow my top." The problems involved are those of denial, the macho image, peer-group pressure, previous experiences, expectations and social conditioning.

In spite of evidence to the contrary, some people still deny that there is such a thing as post-trauma stress. One senior officer in a largely male organization said very firmly, "My men will not suffer from stress of any kind." Another said, "There is no such thing as post-trauma stress except for those with personality problems who do what social workers tell them." He said this with clenched teeth, popping eyes, white knuckles and his breath coming in short pants. Yet another leader said, "Those who believe in post-trauma stress are really trying to persuade people who are involved in disasters or trauma that they owe themselves a problem."

All of these are very powerful denials of the existence of stress reactions. As an extension of this denial we need to examine the effects of the "macho image" on people, especially in male-dominated organizations. The need to maintain a macho image can deeply affect how people respond. Because of this there can be deep suspicion of any approaches which attempt to deal with them. When we look at psychological debriefing we will see that the process does not *suggest* symptoms, but helps people to work through what they *really think and feel*. The focus is put firmly on them and not on the debriefer.

Some people in certain jobs and professions deal every day with what can be really severe stress. Policemen, fire and rescue workers, ambulance personnel, doctors and hospital personnel, clergy and those who deal with death or dead bodies, are all involved on a regular basis with incidents that could be very traumatic for most of us. This does not mean that they are *immune* to the stress, but it can mean that they have become accustomed to it and have developed strategies for coping. Their training and experience usually takes over during the event and enables them to cope. But some might find that the strategies they use are not very effective or helpful either for them or their colleagues and families. This is discussed in chapter 5.

Examples of Reactions
Some further examples of the effects of post-traumatic stress should help us to see that the ways in which it affects people are many and varied although there are some feelings and reactions which are common to them all.

War

A young soldier on leave from Northern Ireland was staying at home with his parents. His mother became increasingly concerned because, she said, he was a changed person. He had nightmares frequently and often woke up screaming and in a sweat. He was drinking heavily and getting drunk regularly, something he had never done before. She would find him wandering around in a state of confusion in the middle of the night.

He was irritable and sometimes couldn't control his anger or temper. She encouraged him to seek help because she believed that this condition was a direct result of what he had experienced in Northern Ireland. He had not witnessed anything terrible or traumatic, but admitted later that he was constantly terrified and afraid that he would be killed or injured. He also said that he couldn't talk to his friends about these feelings, although he knew that some of them felt the same way.

This man's reactions are not uncommon among people who are under constant stress and fear for long periods of time, but who generally manage to keep them under control until later.

A soldier who buried dead bodies in wartime said that the only way he could cope was by getting drunk every night. He said the alcohol dimmed his memories and thoughts and helped him sleep. He added that he was not the only one who tried to cope this way and that it was common among those who had this job.

He claimed that alcohol helped him put aside what he was doing, but after the war he still had disturbing thoughts and feelings about what he had been through. As he talked about this he gradually became more and more upset, until he cried over what he described as "a few dead bodies." He then went on to say that he did not see them as the enemy, but as people who were caught up in something neither he nor they understood. His main response was one of extreme sadness and regret.

Hostages

Judy was held hostage for several weeks with a group of friends. When she returned home with them she was given an opportunity to talk through her experiences and feelings. The others were content to do this. But she went into the group and walked out again after a few minutes. A debriefer who had stayed outside in case this

> happened commented to her that she obviously had not
> felt like going back into the group.
>
> Judy was extremely angry and upset and said that
> she did not need to talk about what had happened. She
> was all right and nothing was wrong with her. Why
> should she need to talk? The debriefer sat quietly and
> listened. Gradually Judy opened up and said she felt that
> she didn't belong in the group even though she knew
> everyone in the group intimately.
>
> She felt isolated and afraid and couldn't even bring
> herself to complete some simple forms. After some time
> she admitted that she felt that she was losing her mind
> and going crazy and would eventually have a nervous
> breakdown. She started by denying that she needed to
> talk . . . and then talked for almost two hours.

Judy was allowed to talk and was reassured that her reactions
were normal. This was an important step in coming to terms with
her feelings of anger, frustration, isolation, loneliness, listlessness
and the fear that she was losing control of her mind.

Trying to avoid feelings rarely works and can cause other,
longer-lasting effects. Keeping away from those who shared the
experience can lead to isolation and loneliness. Paradoxically,
ex-servicemen's organizations and groups formed for survivors of
disasters can have the opposite effect from what was intended. It
also applies to other self-help groups and support organizations.
A survivor of an incident said

> I can be with those who shared the events that caused the
> trauma, but this can isolate me from the rest of the world,
> including my family members, who were not there. While
> I recognize that they do a tremendous job in supporting
> me and many others in and through our problems, it can
> mean that some of us become secure within the group
> and cannot move forward. I feel that I have gone through
> an experience that you, the outsider, do not understand.
> But this can make me feel that I am alone and isolated—
> not just by myself, but with others who belong to this
> exclusive club. It makes me feel special, but even more
> alone, even in the middle of a group of people who have
> shared the same or a similar experience.

Riots

Jeff was a policeman who had been involved in a very
violent and lengthy riot where many civilians were
injured and some of his colleagues hospitalized. About
four days later, he was in a supermarket with his wife
when he suddenly found himself sitting on the floor
surrounded by a crowd of people. He felt that everything
was out of his control and he just wanted to run away
and hide. He was in a panic, was confused and at first
didn't know where he was. As he came to gradually, he
found an older woman with his wife, asking if she could
help him up. He started to laugh, but knew he was hiding
his feelings of embarrassment, inadequacy and shame.

Such experiences can be frightening and disturbing and can
occur days, weeks, months or even years later, or at times when
people think that they have forgotten the incident and have
learned to cope.

Accidents

In the armed services, on police forces, among prison guards and
in other similar organizations, there can be very strong peer-group
pressure not to show emotions or feelings, especially fear.

I remember as a serviceman in the British Royal Air Force
seeing some airmen, who were in the fire service, called
to an aircraft that had crashed on the runway. The pilot
had burned to death in the cockpit. For weeks they
would make signs and gestures when they met and curl
up their bodies, hands and faces at each other and snarl.
Then they would laugh. This was one way in which they
tried to cope with what they had seen. If they made a
joke about it, perhaps they thought it would go away.

Shootings

Sometimes people are killed by the police or the military while
carrying out armed robberies or acts of violence and terrorism.
Even though the police and military have been trained carefully

and the shooting was deemed necessary in order to save life, the reactions can be quite traumatic.

> One man who shot an armed robber to save his own life and the lives of others reacted with the comment, "He could have been my son." He suffered severe shock and guilt. He was angry with himself and with the dead man, and was not sure where to place the blame and guilt. The fact that he had taken a human life was paramount: He could still see the shock, horror and surprise on the face of the man as he shot him.
>
> He was shaking with grief and couldn't cope. He felt that his wife didn't understand what had happened and how he felt. He also felt a sense of isolation and that he had done something unnecessary, although he knew that it was either to be his life, someone else's life or the robber's life. He had acted in a split second and made the decision to shoot when he believed that he was going to die. Facts and calm reasoning, at this stage, did not come into play. Now, however, he felt dreadful and dirty.

There was nothing here of the "Dirty Harry" or "cops and robbers" reaction, where there is a sense that justice has been done and a feeling of satisfaction that a criminal has received what he deserved. The experience is usually extremely disturbing and upsetting, and there can be strong reactions following shootings, even when people have not been killed. "I am trying to save lives, but I might have to take a life. And my own life is at risk."

Bank robbery

> Mike was a bank clerk who was suddenly faced by a masked man with a sawed-off shotgun. The gun was thrust into his neck and face, and he was hit on the head. The man swore and cursed and threatened to kill him unless money was handed over. This ordeal only lasted a few minutes, but Mike was terrified. When the man left, Mike ran and hid in the restroom until he felt able to face the rest of the staff and the police.

A few days later he admitted to a debriefer that the
worst thing for him had not been the fear of being killed
but that when he was being threatened he became like an
animal. "I felt debased and dirty and would have killed
him with my bare hands if I could. I felt just like an
animal and almost pissed my pants. That's how humiliated
I felt. I was disgusted with myself and still am."

Mike was so frightened that he had been unable to protect the
female employees or do anything about the gunman. He was
unable to come to terms with the feeling that he had lost his own
sense of value and self-worth. If he felt he could kill "just like an
animal," what kind of a man was he? How would he have felt if he
had degraded himself further?

Divorce

Post-trauma stress is not confined to disasters and accidents, but
also is common in situations such as divorce and separation. It is
said that the three most traumatic events we can experience, in
descending order, are: bereavement, divorce and moving to
another house. All of these can result in stress and post-trauma
stress. When marriages break up, the result can be loss and trauma
for all involved. Divorce is often tinged with deeply disturbing
feelings of guilt and failure, even when there is relief that an
impossible relationship is over. The sense of relief can increase
guilt feelings and increase the trauma.

When I got divorced, I lost everything. I lost my partner
and what might have been a happy and satisfying
relationship. I lost my house, my home and my children.
Not only that, I lost my self-esteem and dignity through
the whole process: the arguing and fighting, the silences
and the anger, the frustration and sense of failure, the
loss of self-control. I went through the screaming and
shouting, the anger and bitterness, the crying and the
depression. My parents don't even speak to me now. I
lost my in-laws, and many of my friends no longer want
to know me.

> I lost my security and feeling of belonging; I lost my
> status in the community. My neighbors ignore me. When
> I say I'm divorced, people just turn away or feel sorry for
> me. I also lost my job. The humiliating visits to the
> attorney made me feel so bad and dirty; and the fighting
> in court for money and the children seemed so
> mercenary and unreal. When the divorce decree finally
> came through I held it in my hand and just broke down
> and cried. I had failed everyone and I had failed myself. I
> had nothing more to lose; I had lost everything. I was
> afraid of what had happened and frightened of the
> future, and I still don't know who or what I am or where
> I am going. I don't think I'll ever come to terms with it.

This kind of reaction is not unusual and is caused by the stress
and trauma of the experience, especially the deeply disturbing
sense of loss. Such a reaction also applies to many other
experiences of loss in life and we consider it further in chapter 5.

Bereavement

Bereavement is also a traumatic experience.

> Marian was 67 when her husband, Clyde, had a heart
> attack and dropped dead. Strangely enough, she showed
> no reaction at all, other than to act as though nothing
> had happened. She didn't cry or talk about him and
> didn't want others to mention it. At the funeral and burial
> she remained calm and in control, and once the rituals
> were over and relatives and friends had gone, seemed to
> settle down into her normal routine.
>
> Three months later, her dog was killed by a car and
> Marian went to pieces, breaking down with uncontrolled
> grief. Her neighbors and friends who couldn't understand
> said, "Imagine that! She thought more of the dog than
> she did of poor old Clyde." Their reaction was
> understandable, but they were wrong. She had bottled
> up her intense grief and kept it firmly under control,
> afraid of what would happen if she let go. She was never
> one to show emotion, but the dog's death was the last
> straw, which broke through her defenses—and the
> floodgates of grief were opened.

Bereavement results in grief symptoms. Grief symptoms are similar to those of post-trauma stress, because both grief and post-trauma stress are the result of traumatic events. Grief can be brought on by the sudden and tragic death of a child, partner or other loved one, or it can be the

Both grief and post-trauma stress are the result of traumatic events.

result of a slow and expected death following a long illness. Either way, the bereavement still results in grief, although in the case of an expected death the grieving process usually begins in the form of "anticipatory grief" before the death occurs.

Grief symptoms, like those of post-trauma stress, can be experienced before and during the event, as well as after it. This means that the stress reactions are not just reactions after a trauma, but can begin and be identified much earlier.

- *Before the incident.* This could affect someone such as a policeman or soldier preparing to face a potentially difficult or dangerous situation, or someone waiting for his own death or for the death of a loved one. It could affect someone anticipating an accident, disaster or other incident that they can see or know is going to happen.

- *During the incident.* The stress reactions during the incident might be repressed or controlled and never emerge, or they might be experienced and expressed at the time of the incident.

- *After the incident.* The reactions can occur immediately afterward or at a later time, varying from a few minutes to many years later.

The Iceberg Theory

One way of trying to understand post-trauma stress is through the Iceberg Theory (Figure 1, opposite page).

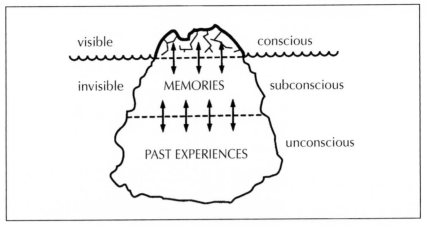

Figure 1. *The Iceberg Theory*

Every human being is like an iceberg floating in the sea, with only a small part visible above the water. The part of the iceberg that rises above the water and can be seen as it floats around in the sea represents our conscious selves. Underneath, hidden from view, is the major section of the iceberg. Similarly, starting just below the surface of our conscious thoughts lies the subconscious. Closest to the surface lie our more recent memories. Certain pieces of information there are immediately available to us and can be recalled instantly when needed: our name, address, telephone number, the place we live in, and so on.

Other pieces of information are more difficult to recall or remember—what we were doing last Wednesday or what we had for lunch yesterday, or the name of the person we met on the bus recently. These can be thought of as lying further under the surface, in the subconscious, but still available when needed if we can remember them.

At a deeper level still lie our unconscious memories and experiences. Some of these we think we have forgotten and would find hard to remember, but a name, a picture, a sound or a smell can bring the memories flooding back.

Deeper still are experiences we have buried and, again, we think, forgotten. The more painful these experiences are, the deeper we have buried them. These can be anything from problems in childhood, concepts of self-worth, what it means to be a man, woman, parent, child, husband, father, mother and friend.

Also hidden away here are things we have done or not done, or that have been done to us, of which we are ashamed or afraid. These, and many other distressing or disturbing experiences, are usually things we do not wish to remember or cannot remember.

We also have buried good experiences, but these are usually more accessible and acceptable to our conscious minds. We also have beliefs, expectations, hopes, prejudices, ideas and a whole "hidden agenda" from our character, upbringing and environment waiting on call, some aspects more deeply hidden than others. Sometimes these can emerge with devastating effect.

> Emma, who was 26 and married, was sitting and listening to some friends talking. The subject turned to child abuse. She wasn't really listening, although she was aware of what was being said. At a break in the conversation, suddenly everyone sat quietly as Emma found herself saying, "I was abused by my stepfather when I was seven." She said that she hadn't known it before. This revelation was almost overwhelming for her and she sought counseling help.
>
> She had been abused, but the memory was so painful that she had locked it away and had forgotten that it was there. Something in the conversation triggered her memory even though she said that she had talked about child abuse generally before without realizing that she was a victim. This experience was traumatic. Counseling proved to be a very painful journey of discovering what she had suppressed, and why, and how it had influenced her life and was causing problems in her present relationships.

Some people do not have such experiences buried away, but live with the pain of them every day. Whether buried or not, these experiences can be very disturbing and will almost certainly influence lives in the present.

Traumatic experiences can lie deep within our minds, and the feelings and emotions associated with them are often all too ready to emerge and influence who and what we are and how we behave. A traumatic event can cause reactions that disturb the "whole iceberg;" that is, the subconscious and the conscious mind alike. Hidden memories and previously learned patterns of coping can be recalled and come to the surface. These may or may not be helpful in the present situation, in which case the feelings and emotions generated by the event can be repressed and pushed down even further. We deny that we are influenced or affected in any way and say that we can cope. Thus when hidden emotions and previous experiences come to the surface, they sometimes make things worse.

If I already have problems relating to attachment, loss and separation from my childhood, and I experience loss in some way or my security is threatened, these old feelings can make it more difficult for me to cope in the current situation. The old feelings have been resurrected into my present life, causing further insecurity and feelings of panic and pain. I may return to the same strategies I used as a child to cope, and these are not likely to be helpful or positive.

In this model, post-trauma stress is *not only* the result of a distressing event, *but also* the result of our own repressed feelings and our own inner world, our previous experiences and the kind of help we are or are not receiving now from other people.

Summary

Post-trauma stress is the development of certain symptoms or reactions following an abnormal event. The event is abnormal in that it is life threatening or extremely disturbing, and can be anything from a minor accident to a major disaster. This includes incidents such as a divorce, riots, war, bereavement or any event that causes trauma and shock. This trauma disturbs our normal life beliefs and turns our world upside down, causing confusion, disbelief, feelings of vulnerability, a loss of meaning and purpose in life, and changes in self-image or self-esteem.

It would not be correct to assume that the symptoms are only found after the event, because they can arise earlier. Seeds of the symptoms of post-trauma stress lie not only in the nature of the event itself, but also in the lives of those who experience it.

Post-trauma stress can result from any experience that, for me, is not normal. Because it is not normal it can cause traumatic reactions. The experience should not be seen as an isolated event but rather as an ongoing situation. I bring myself—my character and personality and previous experiences—to the event. All of these, including the nature of the event, will determine how I react both at the time and later.

> A man walking down a street in front of a group of
> apartments was hit on the head by a falling plant pot.
> This abnormal and unusual event shocked and
> traumatized the man. Later, he suffered from agoraphobia
> (fear of open spaces) and the fear that the same thing
> might happen again if he went out into the street.

Perhaps a trivial accident, it nevertheless caused emotional disturbances as well as physical pain, both at the time and later. We look at the characteristic symptoms of post-trauma stress in more detail in the next chapter.

Further Reading

Hodgkinson, Peter, and Michael Stewart. *Coping with Catastrophe: A Handbook of Disaster Management.* New York: Routledge, 1991.

McManus, Marianne L. *Quake Stress: Preparation for the Psychological Effects of a Major Disaster.* California Psychological Publishers, 1988.

Raphael, Beverly. *When Disaster Strikes: How Communities & Individuals Cope with Catastrophe.* New York: Basic Books, 1986.

The Symptoms

IN THE SAME WAY that grief is a natural, normal reaction to bereavement and loss, post-trauma stress is a natural reaction following sudden or abnormal events in our lives. Stress reactions can occur not only after, but also during the event. The extent of the reaction to the traumatic event depends to some degree on the previous experiences of those involved.

For example, if I have already experienced this particular kind of event and the stress associated with it, and learned to cope with it, then I will probably cope if it happens again. If the experience is new and disturbing, I might have few, if any, strategies for coping and will find little from my previous experiences to help me at the time or later.

As the example above shows, post-trauma stress is not an isolated or unique set of symptoms that is found only after a trigger incident has happened. The symptoms can be present during and after the incident also. We need to take a dynamic rather than a static view of post-trauma stress and see that the roots of its symptoms lie in one's *total experience* of loss. This extends from before the incident happens to its aftermath, which can be weeks or years later. Therefore, to understand the symptoms we must consider the previous experiences, background, character and personality of the person involved, the extent and nature of the traumatic event itself, and the quality of help and support given during and following the incident.

For example, fire and rescue workers are trained to cope with an accident. If they suffer from stress, even at a low level, their training and experience usually enable them to compensate for that and accomplish their work efficiently. A pedestrian passing by at the time of the incident might try to help, but if she has no training or previous experience to fall back on, she probably will not be able to cope well with the stress of the situation.

The rescue worker, in addition, has the support of his colleagues both at the time and later, and might also have the services of a counselor or debriefer available. The pedestrian who tries to help might stagger away from the incident with no support or help from anyone—and so may become another victim of the accident. This person tries to cope and continue, but has no inner or external resources or experiences from which to draw support or strength. The volunteer might experience symptoms of post-trauma stress and actually be at more risk than the rescue worker of developing post-traumatic stress disorder.

It is impossible to say how individuals will suffer or who will suffer most. But through training and experience, and by providing a support system, we can reduce the risks and possible effects. What we cannot do is prevent the incident from affecting us in some way or other, no matter how minor an effect this might be. In fact, the symptoms might be that we show no symptoms whatsoever! The point here is that no reaction *is* a reaction.

No reaction is a reaction.

> I just kept on doing the job I had been trained to do.
> The conditions were] terrible, but I really didn't feel
> anything at all. Others were very upset, but not me. It
> was all in a day's work as far as I was concerned.

That is the way one person responded to a traumatic incident he was involved in. Whether he will have any further reaction is difficult to predict. It might be that he will smoke or drink more than usual, have minor health problems or difficulties at home or work—but then again, he might not, and he may seem to be the same person he has always been.

Being involved in a traumatic incident can disturb our basic life beliefs and result in a struggle to adjust, adapt and survive. This includes loss of the feeling of invulnerability—"I am not immune to disaster; I am mortal." Loss of meaning and purpose in life—"There isn't any point." And loss of self-image—"I am not who I ought to be." The resulting attempts to cope can affect every area of life and are experienced as physical, emotional, spiritual and social losses.

Physical Loss

> John was sitting in the front of a bus when he saw a truck hurtling toward him out of control. Everything seemed to go into slow motion. His first thoughts were, "Oh my God, this can't be happening—but it is. When will it hit us? What can I do? Am I going to die?" These thoughts flashed through his mind in the seconds before the accident. The bus began to skid as the driver took evasive action, but there was a horrible crash, the truck collided with the bus and John's world, literally, turned upside-down.
>
> John was thrown to the floor, and when the bus came to a halt he slowly got to his feet to discover the bus on its side. He could hear people screaming and moaning. He had survived, but was slightly stunned and bruised. There was a strong smell of gasoline and in a panic he began to climb through a broken window, only pausing to help another passenger to escape. Images planted in his mind were of broken metal and glass and bodies. He staggered away from the bus, into the arms of a passing pedestrian.

John's thoughts and impressions were confused throughout this incident.

- *Before the crash*. He was sitting calmly in the bus on his way to work thinking of his family and of going to the movies that night. He was at peace. Then he saw the vehicle out of control coming toward him. He began to panic and felt fear surge inside him as he tried to prepare for what might happen. Was he going to die or be injured? Would he survive?

- *During the crash*. He felt and heard the crash as the vehicles collided. Could he escape? Was he injured? Visual images of the scene were impressed on his

mind—of blood and bodies, twisted metal, broken glass
and the smell of fuel. His thoughts were, "I have to get
out. I have to survive."

- *After the crash.* He wondered what he had done and
what he could or should have done. "Did I do anything
to help others? Was I selfish? Did I fail?" These questions
were combined with feelings of guilt and shame at his
own reactions of fear, panic and self-preservation.

For John, this three-stage process traced his movement from
feeling secure and safe to a rising sense of fear and impending
disaster, and finally into shock, confusion, panic and guilt. This
was not post-trauma stress, but a continuing experience of stress
over a period of time from before the crash took place until it was
over. The crash was over, but not
the experience of stress.

The crash was over, but not the experience of stress.

Previously John felt that he
was reasonably in control of his
life and that most things seemed to
make sense. He knew that difficult things were happening around
him, but he was able to push these thoughts aside and live in his
relatively safe little world. A traumatic incident had disturbed this
view of life. Everything became meaningless and seemingly
without purpose. He looked for a way to restore the balance so he
could make sense of it all once more and, by doing so, be able to
cope and carry on.

All kinds of strange feelings began to churn inside him. He felt
very strongly that part of him had been removed. It was as though
something had been torn out of his chest or stomach. (Similarly, in
cases of bereavement some will say they feel raw, as though their
insides have been scraped out.) For John, it was like being run
over by a steamroller; he had a deep sense of shock. Had he lost a
leg or an arm or fingers or hand in the crash, then the sense of
physical loss would have been even greater.

People who go into the hospital for an operation may
experience a similar feeling of loss. Physical losses are also
experienced when we lose possessions and belongings such as

clothing, money and personal items. We can also lose objects like a house or the familiar sights and scenes around us that help us to feel at home and at ease.

The disaster in the Welsh village of Aberfan in 1966, when a wall of coal slid down onto a school, killed 116 children and 28 adults, and changed the physical face of the village. The destruction of buildings, streets, mountains, forests and rivers can alter our perspective on the world around us—a world on which we depend and which helps us to make sense of our experiences and work out who and what we are as people. Such destruction is experienced as both internal and external loss. Our world is not the same, inside or out.

Emotional Loss

Bereavement

The deaths of family or friends—even strangers, such as fellow passengers—can cause the loss we experience as grief. In the case above, John saw the bodies of other passengers lying around him, and although they were strangers, they added to his feelings of horror and shock. He experienced a deep sense of grief. He had been bereaved and would need to grieve.

Loss of self-esteem and self-image

Because he had climbed out of the bus and left people behind, John believed he had failed. His sense of failure caused a loss of self-esteem: "I could have done more to help others."

This is a loss in that John felt he had not lived up to his idea of himself as a caring and coping human being. He also experienced the loss of his own self-image because he thought that he had failed as a man. "I cannot be a man any more. I behaved like a selfish animal." He had believed himself to be someone who was very much in charge of his own life and who would keep a firm grip on himself, whatever happened. This had been shattered and now he sees himself as less than the person he thought he was. "I should have coped, but I went to pieces."

Loss of purpose and aim

John's life had changed; it no longer seemed to have any meaning. "What's the point any more? Why bother to go on? What's it all about?" The ability to make any sense of his world had been thrown into confusion, and he began to question the reason for living. "How can things like this happen to me and to other people? Everything was going so well, and I was minding my own business on the bus. Surely this is the result of a cruel fate! How can I go on if things can happen out of the blue over which I have no control?" John was forced to question the assumptions he had made about his life and future.

Loss of security

John was suddenly made aware that he is vulnerable. He could have been killed, his wife could have become a widow and his children could have been left without a father. He experienced life as something that was "breakable." "Nothing is certain any more. I can die. I am no longer sure of anything—my life included." John has to try to come to terms with his own vulnerability and, perhaps, his own inevitable death.

No matter how far in the future this might be, the accident seems to have brought it closer. The shock of this accident tipped his whole life into turmoil and confusion, and he could not see any way out of it. He felt angry, guilty, extremely vulnerable, isolated and victimized.

John did not experience this himself, but another potential problem can magnify the stress a traumatic experience causes: These are our past experiences. Our past experiences, our hidden agendas, can be resurrected and cause even further confusion and disruption of our comfortable world at such a moment. The shock, fear and panic we have experienced in previous events may return during a new and traumatic event.

> Margaret worked in a bank and was involved in an
> armed robbery. This was the second time it had
> happened to her, and that made the experience even
> worse. She thought she had learned to cope after the first

incident, but during and after the second robbery, old feelings from the first incident began to return and were almost overwhelming. She could feel the fear and see the barrel of the shotgun all over again. Those memories made her reactions this time doubly difficult to control. On the previous occasion she had repressed the feelings, thinking they had gone away, but they returned with a vengeance and were compounded by her present experiences of fear and shock. She realized that she needed professional help in order to cope with them.

How we learned to cope in the past, and our experiences of disaster and crises, no matter how small or trivial, can come hurtling to the surface at the time of a similar experience. They come sliding up from the depths of our minds where we thought we had them safely locked away. If we coped with similar crises by ignoring them and pretending they didn't happened or were not important, or thought that we ought to cope by being strong, then we will tend to use similar strategies to cope again. Some have more effective and appropriate methods of coping than others. Some will be unable to cope, and others will manage to hang on just barely.

Adrian, a man from London, was involved in a riot as an innocent bystander. A policeman took him to his car. "I just sat in my car and stared into space. I felt confused and frightened, and slowly I could feel images of the air raids from the last war coming into my mind. I could hear the sirens and the explosions of the bombs. All I wanted was to cry and run away. I sat for about half an hour and then slowly drove home. Fortunately I was able to talk this through with my wife and that helped me to calm down and cope."

The area of emotional loss raises the problem of social and family conditioning, especially of the macho image often found in men and in male-dominated organizations. If someone has been brought up to deny or bury his feelings and emotions, then he will probably do so whenever he faces a crisis.

Spiritual Loss

The feeling that our world has been turned upside-down and that life is grossly unfair and unjust can destroy our deeply held beliefs, whatever they might be. It can confirm our conviction that life is a sick joke and that there is no God. Or we might discover a new faith and purpose. Either way, it can mean the loss of what we felt had made some sense of our lives and the world around us. Finding a faith through or in a crisis can be as disturbing as losing one.

Some feel that conversion to a faith should be the result of dramatic and disturbing events, and so it is for some people. For others, similar experiences and events can destroy faith. However, both finding a faith and losing one involves loss, and adjusting to the changes involved can be disturbing and traumatic.

This will be examined further when we look at bereavement and how this can affect belief. Loss of belief can cause depression, dread and a descent into meaninglessness, and the feeling that there is no reason or point in living. In John's case, it meant that he was led to question the meaning of his life.

If you experience an accident, disaster or bereavement, you are not usually in a condition to be able to think things through. You cannot usually be logical or reason things out, and there are no answers to the questions people ask other than those that are generally unhelpful. To say, "It is God's will," or "part of a great plan," or "just one of those unfortunate things," does not help.

Social Loss

An accident or disaster can result in the loss of family and friends. You may no longer have a wife, husband, partner, parent, child or friend. Even if they are alive, whether involved in the incident or not, they might not understand what has happened to you. Their lack of understanding can make you feel isolated and alone, and you may retreat into your own little world.

You might not be able to cope with work after a traumatic incident. You might lose your job and source of income as a result. Work and income, as well as family and friends, give us a sense of purpose. The loss of any of these can result in either looking for a new identity and purpose, or retreating into apathy and inactivity. The influence of family, friends and work are important in helping you to establish your own personal and social identity. When you lose the people around you, you lose those who help you to be who and what you are.

Summary

All of these losses—physical, emotional, spiritual and social—can be experienced when a person is involved in an accident or disaster. They can cause the symptoms of post-trauma stress. However, these losses are not separate compartments of experience, but blend into each other in the complex relationship that exists between body and mind. Each of these affects the others. Loss of a spouse or child in an accident entails physical, emotional, spiritual and social losses, all mixed up in one experience. It can cause intense feelings of grief—shock, anger and isolation, as well as loss of faith and self-worth, and a possible descent into depression.

We cannot tell from just looking at a person what is being hidden away and repressed. There may be little or no evidence of any stress reactions at the time of the incident, but this doesn't mean there aren't any. Those involved in the incident may be completely unaware of their feelings and emotions. Their feelings may or may not emerge later. If they do, they are symptoms of post-trauma stress. The reactions may be found during or soon after the traumatic incident or within a few hours or days.

However, it is not quite as simple as this because the symptoms may not be present or apparent at the time and may emerge months or even years later. These symptoms can be found in a number of experiences, from bereavement or a car crash to a major disaster—but all can be seen as reactions to trauma and loss.

Many other events in our lives result in loss and therefore in similar reactions. These losses are due to the changes we go through as we fight and develop from conception and birth to death: separation anxiety in childhood, going to school, puberty, making and breaking relationships, leaving school and home, starting work, unemployment, falling in love, marriage, pregnancy, miscarriage and abortion, having new children in a relationship, separation and divorce, moving to a new home, hysterectomy, menopause, retirement and adjusting to old age, the death of a spouse and the inevitability of one's own death. All of these, and also natural and man-made disasters, entail loss and therefore involve grief reactions and post-trauma stress.

Characteristic Reactions

While a traumatic event takes place, certain emotional and physical reactions are present, most of which are kept under control, but other specific symptoms can occur once the incident is over. These symptoms are extensions of the experience at the time of the event and are characteristic of post-trauma stress.

They can be found directly after the event or may emerge at a later stage and continue or intensify for some time, at which point they are defined as *post-traumatic stress disorder* or *PTSD*.

In 1980, the American Psychiatric Association published the third edition of a manual entitled *Diagnostic and Statistical Manual of Mental Disorders* (revised 1995). This reference defined PTSD. The condition was recognized previously among victims of concentration camps (as described in Bruno Bettelheim's *The Informed Heart*), Vietnam veterans, and others suffering as the result of violence, disaster, accidents or war.

The disorder develops generally as a long-term reaction to the stress.

However, the feelings, emotions and physical reactions we have described can also be found in post-trauma stress. The *disorder* develops generally as a *long-term reaction* to the stress. That means the symptoms persist, intensify, and cause extreme distress and disruption of normal living as time goes on. We can place the symptoms of post-trauma stress and PTSD under three main headings: *re-experiencing, avoidance* and *arousal.*

Re-experiencing

The trauma-inducing event can be experienced again hours, days, months or even years later. Feelings and emotions that were generated at the time can be felt as if they were happening *now,* in the present. They can vary from being mildly disturbing and upsetting to intense and overwhelming. The sensations and emotions felt at the time of the incident have been repressed into the depths of the mind, but come to the surface when least expected.

Triggered reactions

These feelings can be "triggered" by sights (TV, video, media, news items, movies, photographs, people, talking about it), and by sounds, smells, tastes and touch.

> In 1984, Barry, a health officer in a large organization, was attending a course on bereavement. He was coping well until the lecturer showed a film about the loss of a child. The film began with a short introduction by the producer, followed by scenes from the disaster in England in October, 1966, during which 116 children and 28 adults were killed. A coal-slag heap almost 800 feet high had slipped and engulfed a school and other buildings in a village. Suddenly Barry gave a cry of agony, stood up and ran from the room. A friend followed him.
>
> Later, Barry said that he had been finding the course very helpful and was sitting calmly waiting for the film to begin. The scenes from the village were unexpected and traumatic for him. In 1966, he had been a young miner in the next valley, a member of the rescue team that had gone immediately to help in the disaster. He said that seeing the film made him feel as though he had been hit physically, and emotions he thought had gone were resurrected in a flash. For him, the sights on the screen brought feelings and memories flashing into the present with a force that caused him to scream with pain. This was 18 years after the event.

Clearly, feelings and the returning symptoms can be experienced not just weeks or months, but many years later and may brought about by some unrelated stimulus. They can be extremely frightening, and the fear of losing control or going crazy is not unusual. Complicating that fear is the fear of not knowing when or where such triggers may be encountered. This can lead people to practice avoidance or isolation.

Some people will not watch the news on television or read newspapers in case the old feelings return, while others will avoid friends or those who were involved with them in the incident. Even seeing a policeman or hearing an ambulance can be difficult for those who have been in an accident, because it threatens to bring the past event into the present.

Anniversaries, especially the first anniversary, can bring memories flooding back. This can be made worse by interest in the media or by the publication of books and articles about the event. There may, for example, be an announcement on TV, accompanied by film footage of the incident. Survivors who see these announcements or clippings may suddenly experience feelings they had managed to keep under control. On some occasions, victims will dread an approaching anniversary and become more and more depressed or edgy as the day nears. This can cause problems not only for them, but also for their families and friends.

Spontaneous reactions

Perhaps a more disturbing way of re-experiencing the symptoms is when they are not produced by a trigger, but come "out of the blue" with no apparent external cause. We can imagine what might happen if a survivor of a shipwreck were suddenly confronted by the film *Titanic* on television, a movie in which a passenger liner capsizes, or sees news footage from the scene of another seafaring accident, such as a ferry sinking.

While some might say reactions in this case are understandable and can be traced to similarities between the events, how does one explain the reactions if the survivor is walking down a street or sitting in bed, reading, when the feelings suddenly return? In this case, no external circumstances aroused the symptoms. So, what did?

If we see an external cause, then we can probably understand the reason for the reaction. It doesn't necessarily make the feelings any better or less disturbing, but we can say that we know what has caused them. When the feelings suddenly spring into the present, without a trigger, acceptance of the feelings is very different. Some might feel that they are losing their minds and that they are not normal. Others manage to cope and know that whatever happens, no matter what the cause, the feelings will go away; they will not be permanent.

> Tony had been in a very severe car crash. He was a passenger in the back seat and had survived unscathed. His two friends in the front had been badly injured and all were trapped in the car until rescued by the firemen and police. The other two were unconscious, and although Tony was fully awake he was unable to move. He could smell gasoline and was terrified that a fire would break out and they would be burned to death.
>
> Afterward, his friends recovered fully from their injuries and all went back to the company where they worked. One day, sitting at his desk, Tony suddenly experienced a feeling of dread, which started in the pit of his stomach. He could smell gasoline, and the same panic and fear he had felt in the car returned. Fortunately he had been taught some breathing exercises at relaxation classes he had attended, and he was able to control himself. Gradually the feelings began to disperse.

These experiences are sometimes referred to as *flashbacks*, but they could equally well be called *flash-forwards*. They can emerge gradually or suddenly from our unconscious. They not only seem to take us right back to the event, but also can bring the feelings and emotions—even sights, smells and sounds associated with it—into the present.

We have buried the experiences and the feelings associated with them deep into the recesses of our unconscious and surrounded them with a protective shell. We would rather forget them, but the reality is that they do *not* go away. At certain times, when we are reminded of the incident, or perhaps when we are relaxing and thinking of nothing in particular, the protective shell opens and the feelings and emotions return and slide into the present.

We would rather forget these feelings and experiences, but the reality is that they do not go away.

Similarly, in grief after a death, there is often the belief that you will get over it soon, that the feelings have gone and are buried in the past. They *are* buried, but they have not gone away. They have been incorporated into our general life-map or agenda, and can hover in the depths of our minds waiting for an opportunity to emerge into the present. This can be a disturbing and devastating experience.

Avoidance

Any frightening or traumatic incident can make you very careful about being in the same situation again. If I have been in a train accident, I might be very concerned about traveling by train. A typical response to this natural hesitation is, "Get right back in there and don't let fear conquer you!"—the stiff-upper-lip approach, which sometimes does work. If you fall off a horse or bicycle, then you might be able to get right back on again and conquer the fear.

This can be a good strategy to apply to fairly minor incidents, but might not be useful for someone involved in a more serious accident or disaster. It depends to some extent on

- Your previous experiences

- The nature of the incident

- The amount and depth of fear or other feelings and emotions that the experience generated

- Your capacity to cope

Some people's love of horror stories and scary movies aside, generally we try to avoid whatever makes us afraid or has scared us. Some people develop phobias about spiders, flying, heights, water, open or enclosed spaces, dogs, cats, rats, mice and just about anything else. Similarly, when we have experienced a traumatic incident, we may try to avoid anything that reminds us of the circumstances, such as places, people, pictures or other things that might bring the memories and feelings back into our minds.

A common response to trauma is denial. This response is actually a form of avoidance, especially among men. Our society still tends to bring up little boys not to show emotions. Women can cry, but not men. It is common for men to claim that they do not have fears of any kind, especially if they are "real men."

If we men were to admit we had fears, then our wives, friends, families and colleagues might think that we are stupid, pathetic, cowardly, weak or going crazy. We fear they would also think that we were unable to cope.

A common response to trauma is denial.

Men who belong to uniformed organizations such as the armed forces, the police and prison services, or the fire and rescue services, all of which are dominated by men in positions of leadership, may find this particularly true for them. The macho image is difficult to stand up against when you belong to an almost exclusively male club and have to keep up the image, which goes something like this: "You have to be strong to be a real man. There is no place for wimps in this man's world."

Some, especially those in authority, look at showing personal feelings as revealing weakness or character deficiency. The underlying message is that if you are a man you will accomplish the job regardless of how you feel. This is often true; a policeman can help at a terrible accident and do his job efficiently. He can bottle up his feelings at the time and be violently sick and upset afterward, but that's OK—as long as it doesn't happen in front of his colleagues. This is usually where training is important. Good training can take over and help us cope at the time even if we do have difficulties later.

There is also the fear that if I admit to, or am found to be suffering from, stress, it could affect my future promotion prospects. Few people want their reactions to stress or a traumatic incident to be recorded on confidential reports or personnel documents.

In some cases, those in authority in these organizations may attribute the fact that some of their men suffer from stress as a criticism of their leadership capabilities and see it therefore as a threat to discipline. Leaders who think this way may try to avoid the problems of stress in their ranks by simply denying their existence:

I am in charge here, and if my men suffer from any kind
of stress then it reflects on me as a leader. They are my
responsibility, and if they suffer from stress then it must
be my fault. I must not have given them the training,
confidence and support they needed. It also means that
my superiors are likely to criticize me for this, and it puts
me under stress and threatens my position. There is also
the possibility of the whole thing getting out of hand. We
can't all be under stress at once or nothing would get
done. And we do not want to put ideas into people's
heads. As the leader, I cannot suffer stress; therefore,
there is no such thing.

The biggest problem of avoidance is, it means people deny
their feelings. If I have been through a traumatic experience and
someone asks, "Are you suffering from stress?," I am likely to say
very firmly, "No." I do not want other people to know how I am
feeling. If I am frightened or ashamed or want to be sick, I might
wish to keep this secret. "Do you need any help or counseling?"
is likely to receive the same reply: "No. I'm not affected by it one
little bit."

The problem is, the more I deny it and the longer it goes on,
the less likely I am to acknowledge that anything is wrong. My
defenses become stronger and the feelings are buried deeper in
my mind. I might be able to deny my feelings to others, but in my
own mind, I know I need to express how I feel. If I can do this on
my own by crying or showing anger, or by talking to my spouse or
best friend, or someone I can trust,
this might be enough for me to
work through my feelings.

*I might not show symptoms
for a long time before I
realize that I cannot cope.*

If I cannot express myself in
any way at all, and keep
everything bottled up inside, then the condition will almost
certainly become worse. If the symptoms persist for more than a
month and become more deep-seated and disturbing, I will suffer
from post-traumatic stress disorder. I might not show symptoms for
a long time before I realize that I cannot cope. Or I may be

unaware of the symptoms, but they are present—ruining my marriage and causing my work to deteriorate. The result can be that others seek help either for themselves or for me. In this case, I will need to see a professional counselor, therapist or psychiatrist. However, my defenses may be so strong that they prevent me from asking for help from anyone. Avoidance can therefore be tied in with the "men don't cry" image of our society and the fear of losing control of ourselves, our own feelings or those of others, particularly those for whom we are responsible.

Avoidance can also mean keeping away from anyone or anything that reminds me of the incident, so that I become isolated within myself and feel that I am alone. On the other hand, I might join a support group or club and cling to something, to someone, to a memory or to a group of people who shared the experience. Through this experience I am at risk of becoming even more isolated and lonely, because now I am locking myself into that experience completely, and locking out other experiences and people. Some people may develop a fatalistic view of life and believe firmly that they have little future.

> Life isn't really any use now and, anyway, I don't think I'll live much longer. My marriage is a mess and will probably break up. Also, I don't see much point in working because I might be dead soon.

Others seem unwilling or unable to recall or remember much about the incident and some will say that they do not remember anything and refuse to talk about it.

People who occupy their minds and their lives almost exclusively with the incident practice another form of avoidance. Some keep a diary and live in the past or surround themselves with objects that remind them of the event. Some involve themselves solely with memories and cannot stop talking about the experience. They become stuck inside their own feelings and cannot move forward. This form of avoidance prevents them from living in the present or facing up to reality.

Arousal

Because a traumatic incident sensitizes the nervous system, other symptoms may arise. A traumatic event can make us touchy and jumpy, and our reactions can be erratic and unexpected.

> He's not the same since he returned home. He tells me one thing and means another and denies that he said it in the first place, and then he flies off the handle at the least thing.

This can be very difficult for other people to live with, especially for a wife or husband, children and family or friends and colleagues. There can be an increased sensitivity to noise: The slightest sound can seem like an explosion and cause people to jump.

> Jamie was involved in an accident at work in which two of his friends were killed. He survived but was crushed under failing bricks and trapped for several hours. When he came out of the hospital, his wife thought he was all right, but noticed that he was very different with the children. Before the accident, he would watch television in the evening while they played on the carpet and, as often happened, they would argue and fight over something.
>
> Usually he would laugh and tell them to stop it, and more often than not he would wind up on the floor playing with them. Now he was different. The slightest noise they made would make him twitch and he sometimes shouted at them. Other times he would just get up and go out into the yard and stand there by himself.
>
> His wife irritated him more and more, and any little incident could result in a fight when he would walk out of the house. He had difficulty sleeping at night and often woke up in a sweat. At times he complained of tightness in his chest and thought he was going to have a heart attack. He had not been violent, but showed signs of strain when they argued, and she worried that he might lose his temper.

An overstimulated sense of awareness and arousal can lead to an incapacity to cope with normal events and experiences and a retreat into isolation. There can be outbursts of anger and violence between bouts of silence and a withdrawal into self.

> A soldier who returned from the Gulf War would move from treating his wife like dirt and abusing her verbally, to locking himself in the bedroom for days at a time. He would emerge to apologize, but this didn't last long. His mood would swing from acute depression to a state of elation. His wife tried to leave him a number of times, but he would disable the car in some way in an attempt to prevent her.

There can be an increased sense of anxiety and an obsession with the fact that the incident might have resulted in your own death. You know that you are mortal and might realize that death is closer than ever before. You have seen death face-to-face and you are determined not to put yourself into the same position again.

Another sign of this increased sense of arousal can be the desire to do things on impulse without knowing why.

> Elizabeth's mother died tragically of cancer within a short period of time, and Elizabeth was with her mother when she died. The next morning, she drove into town and bought a very expensive cut-glass vase, which she neither needed nor could afford. When her husband asked her why she had bought it, she said that she didn't know.

Replacement behavior like this is quite common. Some people will spend vast sums of money on things they don't need, change their lifestyle or relationships and do things they have never done before. There can be the desire to move and change jobs, to buy a new car and change one's image, or to travel.

Others can become dissatisfied with their relationships and look for what they perceive of as a new and livelier partner. Marriages can break up. It is sometimes a case of, "off with the old and on with the new." The effects of this can be devastating to the person concerned and to their families and friends, but they might not think that they are doing anything unusual: "Life is short, so I might as well get as much out of it as I can. What's wrong with that?"

Re-experiencing the event, avoiding reminders, elation and arousal are typical symptoms of post-trauma stress. They may or may not be evident at the time of the incident, but can return months or years afterward, sometimes with devastating effect.

Further Reading

American Psychiatric Association. *Diagnostic and Statistical Manual of Mental Disorders*. Washington, D.C.: American Psychiatric Association, 1995.

Hodgkinson, Peter, and Michael Stewart. *Coping with Catastrophe: A Handbook of Disaster Management*. New York: Routledge, 1991.

Reactions

FTER A TRAUMATIC INCIDENT, the urge to deny one's feelings about what happened can be very strong. Those who use this emotional defense will usually say that they do not need help and that they are coping well.

> Some men who were involved in the last war, and were all taken prisoner together, came home when the conflict was over. Most were held in the same prison camp, although some were separated from their friends on purpose by the enemy. On their return, they were gathered together for a presentation on the possible effects of their experiences on them and their families. When it was over, they offered no comments or questions whatsoever.
>
> In fact, these men made it quite clear that they were all coping and adjusting and were not suffering in any way. Their strongest defense arose when it was mentioned that they might have difficulties with sex. There was a general round of laughter, and they said none of them had any problems in this area of their lives. One member stood up immediately after the presentation was over, thanked the presenters, looked at the audience and said that they were all coping quite well and would not need any help. There were grunts and nods of approval at this very positive ending!

It seems highly unlikely that a large number of men can suffer confinement, fear and separation from their wives for a long time without at least one of them having some problems, whether sexual or not. However, what man would admit that he had such problems in front of his friends and in public? This is the natural expression of the denial defense.

Feelings

Many feelings can emerge after a traumatic event.

Sense of pointlessness

Some will say very firmly, "Why bother? Why go on?" "There doesn't seem to be any reason to go on." Life has lost its meaning. Some people will be unable to work or sustain relationships. Their marriages can become very difficult or end in separation and divorce.

Increased anxiety and vulnerability

Being involved in an accident or disaster, or losing someone you love, can result in strong feelings of anxiety and worry. You realize that you might have died or been injured or maimed. This can cause panic and fear, but also intense sadness or, worse still, depression and a descent into apathy and inactivity.

Intrusive images and thoughts

People can see images of the event flashing into their minds, or these can be projected outside. They can see faces and bodies, mangled planes, cars or trains, and even experience smells and sounds that remind them of the event.

After a disaster in which many buildings were destroyed, one man said, "I will never forget the smell of wet smoldering wood mingled with stale sweat and the smell of food cooking."

Thoughts can also intrude: "Why didn't I do this or that?" or "If I hadn't done that, then this wouldn't have happened." *Maybe, perhaps, possibly, if only, might have, could have, should have, ought to have, didn't, couldn't, wouldn't, shouldn't*—all these thoughts can intrude into our thoughts, and we begin to question almost everything we or others did during and after the event.

The images can be disturbing because sometimes they seem to bear no relation to what we have been through. Like dreams, they can be full of weird and seemingly unconnected pictures, people and scenes.

Nightmares and sleep disturbances

If I have intrusive thoughts and images, and especially if I refuse to acknowledge how I really feel, then these thoughts can also be experienced in dreams and nightmares. Perhaps my natural defenses are down when I am asleep. The thoughts and images will not stay hidden because they need to emerge. These can be anything from mildly disturbing to extremely frightening, and can cause people to wake up in a cold or a hot sweat, sometimes shouting or screaming and wondering where they are, even thinking that the event is happening all over again.

The thoughts and images will not stay hidden because they need to emerge.

> After the Gulf War, a soldier said that he often had nightmares, and when he woke up in a sweat in the middle of the night, his wife would call him a "pain in the ass" and say, "Not again. What's wrong with you?" She didn't understand his problem and felt that he ought to be able to cope.

People may suffer disturbances in sleep patterns or be unable to sleep, rest or relax. Some ask their doctor for sleeping pills.

Shame, anger, regret, blame, guilt and bitterness

Some people may have feelings of shame because of real or imagined behavior: "I could have or should have done something to prevent it or to help. I didn't behave like a man."

Anger is common. Anger is a natural reaction to trauma and loss and can be directed at anyone, self included: "Why me?" "Why him?" "Why her?" An extension of anger is the desire or need to blame. Again, this can be directed at anyone and everyone: God, those in authority, the doctor, the minister, social worker, policeman, and many others—all can be blamed for what has happened.

Tied in with blame is the feeling of guilt. Directing blame onto other people or events can seem satisfying, but it is also natural to blame oneself. This causes guilt and further anxiety, sometimes in a vicious circle: "I blame you, so I feel guilty for blaming you, and this makes me feel even more guilty than I did before. And because I feel guilty, I feel the need to blame someone, so I feel more guilt . . ." and so on. I can even blame the one who has died for being so inconsiderate as to die. This escalates the cycle of anger, blame and guilt even further. This reaction is as likely to occur after a bereavement as it is with post-trauma stress.

> *How could he do this? We were going on our vacation next week.*
>
> *If he'd lived longer we would have had a better pension.*
>
> *I hate her for dying. It should never have happened. I get so angry with her that sometimes I scream with rage.*

Blaming the person who has died can be expressed in much stronger words and expletives not printable here, but it is a natural, normal expression of anger and frustration at the loss. This can also apply when we are in an accident or disaster with someone else.

The blame and anger can be directed at fellow passengers, especially those who have been killed, even if we did not know them. Bitterness is also common, and there can be a deep cynicism and resentment about work, family friends, self or life in general.

Survivor guilt

Perhaps difficult to understand is the feeling of guilt at having survived. It is like a two-headed coin, because "I am glad I am alive and that it wasn't me who died, but it makes me feel guilty that I am glad to have survived when others didn't. Sometimes I might feel that secretly I really wanted someone else to die, and that I didn't care who died as long as it wasn't me." This intensifies the personal feelings of guilt and raises other questions.

> Why did I live? Why didn't I die instead? I shouldn't be here. I should be with them/him/her. A real human being (or man, leader, policeman, rescuer, father, mother or whomever else) wouldn't wish someone else to die instead of them. This makes me feel terrible.

This conflict can even apply to those who were not present at the time of the incident. Some who stayed behind during wartime were thankful not to be in danger, but felt guilty because they were not with their friends and comrades, especially when some were killed or injured. You can feel guilty, and even angry, that your partner or child has survived when someone else's has been killed. "Her baby died and mine lived. Why?" "Her husband was killed in the war and mine came home. This makes me feel terrible."

These feelings may cause people to avoid those who have suffered a loss, behavior for which they feel even more intense guilt. Some people retreat into social isolation and loneliness. It might seem strange that it can be difficult to face life when others have suffered so much and you haven't. People may use words like *fate* and *luck* and they may attribute their lives and fortunes on these forces. Some may attribute what happened to divine action or intervention and turn to religion for comfort and absolution.

Sense of isolation and loneliness

Being involved in an accident or disaster can be terribly isolating. We have experienced something awful and feel that nobody else understands—even those who were involved in the same incident. This is true in the sense that your experiences are unique to you. Even if someone was with you at the time, that person is different, with different life-patterns, expectations and backgrounds. Therefore each person's experiences of the same event might be similar, but they are not the same. If you have a baby who dies at three months and I lose my baby at three months, it is easy to think that we both know how the other person feels. The fact is, we *don't* know. We share something in common, but our reactions and feelings might be different in kind or intensity.

"Nobody understands how I feel or what I went through" is a common reaction. One method of coping is to retreat into isolation or to join a select group who shared the experience. Yet belonging to such a group can also increase the sense of isolation and loneliness.

Fear of closed or open spaces

In response to a traumatic event, some will confine themselves to their home and suffer from agoraphobia, the fear of open spaces. Others will find it difficult to be confined, even in their own homes. They develop claustrophobia, a fear of closed spaces. They do not want to go to their office or place of work or sit in a confined space, such as a car. This is especially true in the aftermath of incidents in which people are trapped or restrained in any way. Open or enclosed spaces can cause feelings of panic and fear and the belief that the incident is happening again. They can trigger the feelings and emotions from the original incident and cause re-experiencing or flashbacks. Because of this, some will try to avoid whatever might remind them of the traumatic experience and possibly trigger a flashback.

Fear of crowds can be another expression of a fear of being enclosed, and so avoiding crowds is another way of avoiding a repeat of a situation that has caused trauma. Groups of people can be seen as threatening or hostile. Likely places to experience this kind of fear is on busy streets, in supermarkets, churches and any place where crowds or groups of people gather. Experiencing this fear can result in further isolation and loneliness.

Fear of the same thing happening again

This is a natural, normal reaction, because if something has happened to me once, it can happen again, even if the possibility is fairly remote. In some contexts, such fear serves a useful purpose: The child who burns its fingers will not be as likely to play with matches again. But the plane-crash survivor who refuses to fly again shows a form of avoidance behavior that can prevent a return to a normal way of life. There is nothing wrong even with this unless it becomes incapacitating or so disturbing we can no longer cope with it.

Behavior
Inability to make decisions

Making even simple decisions can be difficult. "Don't ask me to fill out any forms or answer any questions, because I can't do it." "I just don't know what to do. I can't make up my mind." This can apply to the most seemingly trivial and unimportant tasks. When you have been through a traumatic experience the simple and ordinary things of life pale when compared with what has been experienced. The effect on people who were once decisive and direct may be that they now find it hard to make decisions or know what to do. They might be unable to say what they want, or why they seem confused or apathetic.

Impulsive actions

This was mentioned earlier in this chapter and applies to bereavement as well as to accidents and disasters.

Irritability and lack of concentration

Some find it difficult to concentrate for any length of time and become irritable.

> A student involved in a car crash found that he couldn't concentrate on his work either in lectures or at home. Friends said that they would find him sitting in classes just staring into space.

An inability to concentrate can lead to more irritability and anger, which is likely to affect all relationships—at home, at work, with friends—and cause marriages to break down and relationships to end.

Anger and violence

Someone who was quiet and reserved can become aggressive and unreasonable, sometimes for no apparent cause. A young man can become aggressive with his friends, and a husband might turn on his wife or children. There may even be violence in a marriage.

This can lead to separation and divorce or to child abuse. This anger can also be directed at animals and pets. Some people may even destroy personal possessions or direct their anger at things such as furniture, cars, television sets or anything else, and sometimes at objects that remind them of the event.

Sleep disturbances

Dreams and nightmares, as well as an inability to sleep or relax, can be common. These are discussed above under "Feelings," but they are also problems of behavior in that they can result in pacing around during the night, shouting or screaming, sweating, panic and fear.

Retreat into isolation

Someone who was gregarious and sociable may become introverted and withdrawn. He may cut himself off from family and friends. He may neglect his appearance and become scruffy, unkempt and dirty. This retreat into isolation is also discussed above under "Feelings," but obviously has an effect upon behavior also.

Physical Effects
Illnesses—minor and major

A traumatic event may trigger illnesses of a nonspecific nature, such as headaches, stomachaches, pains or tightness in the chest and various pains in other parts of the body. Doctors might find that patients return over and over, complaining of certain symptoms when nothing appears to be wrong physically. The symptoms may be real or imagined, but should not be dismissed as the reactions of a hypochondriac.

Doctors need to consider the possibility that the patient has been through an incident or event such as an accident, disaster, loss or major change in their lives. This applies to all traumatic incidents and includes the other losses in life discussed in chapter 5, such as moving, being laid off, divorce, separation, getting married, being pregnant, having a baby and retirement.

Listlessness

Some complain of never having any energy, of being tired all the time: "I feel washed out and exhausted. I just can't make myself do anything." This might result in neglecting a home, children, partner, work or self.

Excitement and hyperactivity

The opposite of listlessness can occur. Some become greatly excited and hyperactive, often with no real aim in life, but may become involved in charity and volunteer work or anything that takes their energy or activity. Others become obsessed with work or a hobby and throw themselves into these to the exclusion of most other things, including their families. There can also be an inability to rest, sleep or relax.

Increased or decreased physical or sexual desire

Some people become very clinging and demanding in their need for physical and sexual comfort, while others retreat into themselves and lose any apparent need for love or affection. This can be disastrous in a marriage or relationship, especially when the behavior is different from the norm. Either way, this can be very disturbing both for the individual concerned and for their partner and family.

> I used to be so loving and affectionate, but I just can't seem to be bothered any more. Maybe I'm just a horrible and unloving person who doesn't or can't care about anything or anyone.

> He's not the same person. He is so demanding and aggressive in our love life that it just puts me off completely, and then he gets annoyed and upset.

It might even be:

> She didn't bother much before this happened, but now she just wears me out.

Increased smoking or drinking

Those who do not smoke or drink might start to do so, and those who increase their intake of nicotine or alcohol may affect their health, relationships, money and work. A few might turn to drugs. If I am depressed and tired, I might believe that drugs can give me a "lift." They might do so temporarily, but taking any kind of drug may result in dependency and addiction and cause personal, social, health and financial problems.

Changes in Values and Beliefs

Loss of faith and purpose

When someone has been through a traumatic incident and suffers from stress, he can change his views and beliefs dramatically, especially if he has lost family or friends in an accident or disaster: "What's the point of marriage, having a family and a job?" or "There isn't a reason any more. It's all a waste of time." People and things that were important become trivial, insignificant and unnecessary. On the other hand, some become clinging and dependent and lose their sense of personal identity and self-worth.

Problems with relationships

Values and relationships can also be affected in the wake of a traumatic event. Marital breakup is possible as a result of the changes post-trauma stress can bring. Spouses, if they were not involved directly in the incident, can ignore the experiences or not understand what their partner is going through. Even if they were there and also suffered stress, they are unlikely to perceive what happened in exactly the same way. They also are unlikely to suffer in exactly the same way. As with bereavement and grief, post-trauma stress can cause people to drift apart and break up relationships between families, relatives and friends.

Some people are brought closer together by trauma and loss, but it is common for the opposite to happen. One person can react in certain ways while the other shows very different responses, and this can make them drift apart. They are unlikely to share the same feelings because they will suffer in their own individual ways.

A woman might look for what she sees as "a more exciting man than this depressed person I am living with." The man can react by saying, "Why should I stay with this jerk?" A person who is looking for more love and affection may it find it difficult to get from someone who is traumatized. As has been said above, a lack of interest in sex *or* a renewed vigor and need for physical affection can be byproducts of a traumatic event. Unless this happens to both partners at the same time and in the same way, problems can occur.

Finding or deepening faith and purpose

Post-trauma stress can influence and affect belief, especially religious belief. Some will discover a new faith, whatever that might be, while others will lose whatever faith they have. Some will be confirmed in their belief that life is without an ultimate purpose, or is the result of chance or luck—or is even the result of evil forces at work in the world.

Some cling to and deepen their faith, sometimes in the face of everything that seems to go against it, while others will move through their problems with dignity and calm, displaying a firm hold on reality and on their own lives. The symptoms of post-trauma stress are similar to those of grief and loss, and are typical reactions to events that are outside the normal range of our experiences.

The roots of these symptoms lie in the complicated relationship that exists in the interaction between the individual concerned, their previous experiences, the nature of the incident and the support he or she received at the time and later. In order to examine this further, we need to look at the nature of loss and its influence on our lives from birth to death. This is the subject of the next chapter.

Further Reading

Bettelheim, Bruno. *Informed Heart: Autonomy in a Mass Age*. New York: Free Press, 1960.

Life, Loss and Trauma

TO UNDERSTAND THE NATURE OF TRAUMATIC STRESS, we have to look closely at the experience of loss. Loss is one of the central experiences of all human life and is included in every aspect of existence—from conception to death. From the beginning of life every human being moves from one stage of growth to another in a gradual process of change.

Growing means that we move from what we have been to what we are now and, hopefully, on into the future to what we will or can be. This process involves loss because we cease to be what we were; something has gone, and something new is taking its place.

Loss is one of the central experiences of all human life.

We are not just "human beings" but "human *becomings*," for life is not static but dynamic. It requires constant and continuing growth, change and decay. Slowly we are becoming someone new in an ever-changing process, which inevitably includes loss. This loss is experienced as traumatic, either in grief or in the reactions of post-trauma stress.

It might be trauma through the joy and exhilaration of winning a race, because even if this gives enjoyment and pleasure, it can also cause pain and physical discomfort. It is not uncommon to feel a "let-down" or depression after a highly charged physical or emotional experience. This can be in the form of mild shock or sadness and a feeling of emptiness. We build ourselves up for it and suddenly it is gone, it is all over.

We are not just "human beings" but "human becomings."

A vacation is potentially a highly stressful event. The preparation, waiting for a train, bus or an airplane, new surroundings, different weather, language, people and food, and the many other differences and pressures can cause stress, resulting in anger, arguments, disagreements, frustration and regret. Some vacationers will return exhausted and upset about the whole experience, glad to be home, but also disappointed because the vacation is over.

It might be the trauma of having to relate to new people, a new job or a new challenge, or it can be the tragedy of bereavement, divorce or moving, said to be the three most traumatic experiences we can have.

Whatever these changes, whether experienced as good or bad, they involve loss as we move from one state, which is familiar and to which we are adjusting, to one that is unfamiliar and sometimes deeply disturbing. The process of living involves constant growth. If we can understand some of the effects that these inevitable changes cause, we can see how the elements of loss they contain relate to the way that stress emerges and traumatic reactions occur.

Birth and Bonding

From the moment of birth, the first problem we face is that of leaving the womb and severing the contact we have with our mother through the umbilical cord. We emerge into the world naked and vulnerable, relying totally on someone else for our existence. Our basic needs are for food, warmth, protection and physical contact; without these, we would die. At the moment of entering the world, we experience loss—loss of the security, warmth, comfort and sustenance provided in the womb by our mothers. In the most terrible and traumatic moments of life, when people are threatened by death, when imprisoned or tortured, they may curl up into a fetal ball, perhaps in the desire to escape from pain and fear and return to the safety of the womb from which they came.

As we grow and develop, we continue to cope with change and loss. Early in life we cling to our mothers for the touch and closeness, known as *bonding,* that provides for our needs. This bonding is the essential eye-to-eye contact and skin-to-skin touch of mother and baby, which some would argue is the strongest bond of affection and love we can ever experience. This can also occur with a substitute for the physical mother, such as a father, nanny, nurse, relative, foster parent or adoptive parent.

Separation and Abandonment

We exist in this utter closeness to mother and, hopefully, are held and hugged, cuddled and loved, as well as fed when we are hungry. Ideally, mother supplies all our needs, but at some early stage we experience what can be a frightening and devastating event—mother is not there when we want her. We wake up and she is not there, so we scream and yell for attention. We may cry from hunger, pain or gas. The loss we experience when mother is absent can bring with it a terrifying sense of abandonment. Some would argue that this experience can permanently influence our whole lives through "separation anxiety" and can produce anger, frustration and rage from deep within.

We are abandoned and vulnerable. We have lost not just our mother, but part of ourselves, and that threatens our very existence. This can cause bad feelings and intense pain emotionally, but because these are so threatening, the baby projects them onto the outside world and, in some cases, onto the mother. This projection can have a dramatic effect on the way the baby views him- or herself. Projecting bad feelings to the outside world makes the baby feel better, but the outside world can then become a frightening and fearful place. The baby's own self-image and esteem and how he or she relates to the outside world can be damaged. It can mean that when the baby (or the child) becomes the adult who faces fear and trauma, his ability to adjust and cope is impaired because of pre-existing inner conflicts.

Those who have a low self-esteem or a lack of self-worth are likely to have these and other feelings intensified if they are involved in a traumatic incident in which they experience the normal loss and trauma reactions of fear, threat, anger, self-blame, guilt, isolation, loneliness, loss of identity and depression.

The Wider World

At the next stage of life, we begin to realize there is more in the world than "mother and me," for the two of us are seen as one person. Other people exist in an ever-widening circle: from father and siblings to a host of strangers peering at us, holding us and demanding our attention. Gradually we begin to explore this external world through our eyes and mouth, through touch, hearing and smell, until eventually we can crawl around and discover an even wider world around us.

These are tremendous experiences of adventure and excitement that are also frightening and new, and therefore involve a sense of loss. Although we grow in confidence and strength, we are moving out and away from the safety of our mother-and-baby oneness. We begin to realize that not only are we separate and separated from mother, others are also impinging on our world. Somehow, in order to exist, we have to learn to cope with those influences and the change they bring with them.

This change in our lives is an experience of loss and can be deeply disturbing. We are moving from the all-enclosing experience of the womb—where we are totally surrounded, held and protected—to a bond with mother that is slowly being threatened as we grow and develop. We move toward the realization that in order to be ourselves and survive we have to include others in our world. How we cope with this loss determines in some measure how we cope with other losses and traumas in our lives.

Teddy Bears and Toys

The move away from total dependence on mother is a traumatic and disturbing experience. In order to cope, we use different strategies to protect ourselves from too sudden a change. One of these involves the use of objects to help us through the transition from clinging closely to mother to coming to terms with the frightening outside world.

These objects are referred to as *transitional objects;* the more well-known examples are teddy bears and soft toys or blankets. In touch and smell these remind us of, and maintain the contact with, that lost period of security and bliss when we felt we were joined

with our mother. The comforter can be a thumb or finger.
Sometimes we see a little boy or girl, or even an older child,
waddling or walking along dragging a piece of blanket or cloth,
sucking a thumb, with a forefinger rubbing the side of the nose.

This fascinating picture is a powerful symbol of attachment
and loss but shows quite clearly a child trying to integrate with and
adjust to the outside world. When we do this, as children we are
reaching to the outside world, but also we are reaching deep
inside ourselves in an effort to cope. A gradual change is imposed
upon us, from the security and safety of mother to realizing that
we must move out and onward in the process of discovery.

It is in this process that we begin to find out who and what
we are. Transitional objects provide the essential links between
our inner world and the world around us. Some psychologists
believe that the most formative period of our lives, especially with
regard to this experience of loss and its influence, is the first six
months of life.

Others argue that the period is shorter or longer than six
months or occurs at an earlier stage, even during the time spent in
the womb. If true, then it can be frightening to think that there are
early experiences in life that are buried away, and perhaps of
which we are unaware, which will influence how we react when
we face loss through involvement in a traumatic incident or events
such as a bereavement, accident or disaster.

Growing Up and Away

Further trauma awaits if we have to take second place to an older
or younger brother or sister and so lose our place in the family.
When we go to kindergarten or school, we have to learn to relate
to even more people. Then there are aunts and uncles, cousins and
grandparents, neighbors and family friends in an ever-widening
and confusing circle.

We grow from childhood through adolescence to adulthood,
experiencing and carrying a whole series of losses with us. We
gain in knowledge, skill and experience, but lose something of the
intimacy and closeness we have known and perhaps still desire.
Meeting new people and situations means that we are forced to

share ourselves and our lives further in order to grow and develop. Growing physically can be quite a shock, especially when we suddenly feel that this is beyond our control and that we will never be the same again.

> I still remember the anger and frustration I felt at the age of nine when I realized that I could no longer fit into the toy cars at the county fair. These were not the roadsters, but enclosed coupes where you sit completely inside. I can still feel that sense of deep disappointment and anger. Now I see it as part of the difficult process I was going through of growing up and away from childhood and learning to accept and cope with growth and loss.

As children, we experience bereavement and loss when we lose toys and teddy bears, but we also lose pets, relatives and friends. Through these experience we know the pain of grief. The commonly held view that children do not grieve and should be protected from it must be wrong, because loss is already an integral part of their lives. Going to school for the first time is an exciting event, but means facing something new. "You're no longer a baby. You're a big girl now." We have moved to a new experience outside the safety of home with a host of people of all shapes and sizes, sometimes friendly and helpful, but other times hostile, threatening and aggressive.

Adolescence

In adolescence and puberty, we move in the slow and painful transition from being a child toward adult life. We are becoming someone new and different. We increase in strength and gradually become aware of our own sexuality. Although this is normal and natural, it means some degree of loss because we have moved from the relative safety of childhood to new and unfamiliar territory. The body of a young and growing man or woman also contains the mind and experiences of a child.

The process of physical and emotional development involves the challenge of change and growth, but also includes the pain and trauma of loss. Other losses in adolescence are also difficult to accept and work through. We may experience rejection by losing girlfriends and boyfriends, have experiences of making and breaking relationships, leaving school, going to college or a university and starting work. All of these are normal, but can be difficult to cope with and may cause stress.

Adoption

For some, there is the discovery that they were adopted and this can be a very painful experience: "I am not who or what I thought I was." There can be the search for lost parents in an attempt to rediscover the roots of our personality and self-hood: "Where do I come from and who am I?" This may cause problems about self-worth and value with feelings of guilt, rejection, anger and depression. "If this can happen to me, then I must deserve it. Even if I don't deserve it, it means that somebody must been mad at me. I feel picked on, victimized and angry."

Starting Work

Starting a job is a major step in our lives, because we are brought up to believe that having a job not only confers money, but also status and dignity. It means learning to relate to new people and a different environment. It involves a new pattern of living, with a great deal of change and adjustment. If I am suffering from post-trauma stress, the reactions I have to this major adjustment might be so strong that I take a number of days off "sick," or am unable to cope with work. This can affect my work or studies and eventually my career, causing further problems so that any of the effects I feel or experience are deepened and exacerbated.

Learning to Love

When we fall in love, we experience deeply disturbing feelings, and although this can be stimulating and exciting, it indicates that we are moving from our single state to the possibility of a new relationship. This can mean a tremendous upheaval in our lives and result in the heights of joy and acceptance or the depths of sadness and rejection. Loving always includes the inevitability of losing that which we love. If I feel constantly rejected and alone, this will influence the way I react to trauma and loss.

Families and Children

Being pregnant, having a miscarriage, stillbirth or abortion are all events that mean a change of state and therefore of loss and possible trauma. When children come into a family, those involved have to learn to relate in new ways and adjust. A father can feel threatened by a new baby, who might be seen as a rival for the love and affection he saw as his exclusively.

> Once there were just the two of us to think about, but now we are three, and we have to include someone else in everything we do. It isn't the same. Things have changed and I feel angry and upset about it.

As families grow and expand, they can include many complications and varieties, from the so-called nuclear family of mother and father plus two-point-something children, to single-parent families, stepparents, stepbrothers or sisters, foster parents and families, adoptive parents, children's homes and extended families. These can be immensely supportive and caring, but are also providers of stress and trauma. Patterns learned in the house and family will influence our capacity to cope with loss, trauma and stress. Our responses will be partly conditioned by the interaction between the way we have been brought up and the environment.

Divorce

Next to bereavement, divorce is said to be the most traumatic experience we can have. When a marriage ends in divorce, or a relationship breaks up, the result is loss and trauma. There are often feelings of guilt and failure, even when an impossible or destructive relationship has ended. It causes trauma for parents, children and extended families and can even be seen as a loss for the whole of society because the stability of the community seems threatened. There can be deep anger and resentment as well as feelings of rejection, failure, guilt, isolation, loneliness and depression. Again, the way we experience these will affect how we respond to a later trauma.

Graham's divorce came through shortly before he was
involved in a car crash where he was injured. He already
felt a sense of guilt, loneliness and failure, and because
of similar feelings resulting from the accident, these were
intensified and more difficult to cope with.

Retiring and Growing Old

Retirement from work and growing old are also major changes in
the development of our lives and involve loss. We generally
believe that work gives us a sense of purpose and worth and when
we retire all this changes.

When I retired I felt lost. One day I was somebody and the
next I was nobody. I just sat at home not knowing what to
do. My job was an important part of my life and made me
feel useful. I had a good income and lots of colleagues and
friends in the firm. Now there's just me and my wife, and
she's as lost as I am. She gets annoyed at having me
hanging around the house, getting under her feet, and we
argue a lot. I feel useless and now realize that I'm getting
old. Now I just draw my Social Security! What a waste.
What a loss. It makes me so angry and resentful.

However, this feeling of being useless and redundant is not
always as strong as this man's, and many people seem to retire
gracefully. Nevertheless, retirement is still a loss and some
readjustment is necessary.

Menopause and having a hysterectomy, which may occur at
around the same age as a typical retirement, are also experiences
of change and loss. For some women, they bring in difficult and
traumatic times involving feelings of bitterness, anger, guilt,
redundancy and shame.

Growing old can cause similar reactions, which may be more
difficult to cope with if an elderly person is involved in an incident
that causes further trauma.

Death and Bereavement

The death of a child, partner, parent, relative or friend is seen as
the deepest loss of all. For some, one of the deepest fears we can

have is the knowledge and prospect of our own death and the dread that this can bring. Some take a fatalistic view, and others find hope and strength through religious or other beliefs. It is said that we only truly become ourselves when we can face the fact of our own death.

> *It is said that we only truly become ourselves when we can face the fact of our own death.*

This can bring acceptance and peace, but many will rage against the reality of their own approaching end. To know that everything you are familiar with will be taken from you is perhaps the final loss that we experience, whether in the death of a partner, child or friend, or in preparation for dying and death itself. This rage against the fact of death gives a clue as to how we can cope with trauma and loss, and will be discussed when we consider bereavement and grief.

When we experience major life changes, war, accidents or disaster, fear can lie at their heart—the fear of dying, of illness or injury, of hurt and rejection. Our lives have been threatened by something we do not understand and cannot control. We find that we have feelings and emotions that are unfamiliar and extremely distressing. At the center of this experience is the experience of loss. Something has happened to us and we have to exist with it. We have lost what we are, or thought we were, and have to try to survive as we are now.

All of these experiences in life, from conception and birth to the grave, will influence and mold the person we are at each stage in our lives. The nature-versus-nurture argument is relevant, for there seems little doubt that we are a combination of both as they interact throughout our lives. Positive experiences will usually be helpful in enabling us to adjust to change and loss. Negative ones may inhibit our ability to cope and survive successfully.

The positive side is that these experiences bring with them the challenge to move onward, to grow and to emerge in the end as much stronger people. However, the negative side is that this challenge also includes the possibility of stress reactions, whether sooner or later, of shock, unreality, anger, blame, depression, fear, guilt, loneliness, rejection, low self-esteem, loss of identity and isolation.

When these negative reactions occur after a traumatic incident, the way we deal with them will be partly conditioned by our previous life experiences. If we have difficulty in coping with or accepting feelings and emotions such as these already, they will almost certainly be compounded and made worse. This applies not only to victims and survivors, but also to helpers, rescuers, carers and the wider circle of family and friends, all of whom can be affected by the event.

Loss and Trauma

The loss reactions experienced as post-trauma stress are similar to those of grief and it will help us to have a wider understanding of them if we look in more detail at bereavement and loss.

The experience of loss

Losing my car keys has almost become a habit, and each time I lose them I experience the same feelings. I am annoyed that it has happened, angry at not being able to remember where I had them last, and frustrated at the sheer inconvenience of it all. I cannot believe that I have lost them, but I search my pockets and briefcase over and over again. I look everywhere in the office or house and hunt high and low for them.

Perhaps I left them on the desk, or they have slipped down the side of the chair? I even want to blame someone else. Has my wife moved them? [Is it her fault?] Have the children been playing with them? [Where can they be, for they must be somewhere?] Tied in with these feelings is a sense of anxiety I will be late for work and for my next appointment.

I even feel guilty about losing them. I go through this turmoil of feelings and run around, and have other people running around, until I find them. If I don't find them, I might sit down for a while and ask, "What's the point of it all? Why bother?"

I could scream with anger, but fall back into despair and inactivity. When I do eventually find my keys, I feel a great sense of relief and satisfaction and can get on with my life. On one occasion I found my keys in the deep freezer with a book I had been reading.

I was sure it must have been my wife trying to convince me that I am going crazy! This is one of life's minor inconveniences, but if I can feel such emotions over the loss of a set of keys, how much more will I feel when I lose a friend, parent, wife, husband or child, or if I am involved in an accident or disaster and face fear and death?

Throughout our lives we attach ourselves to various things and people around us and these become necessary and familiar parts of our lives. Indeed, some of them become part of us and make us who and what we are both inside and out. They become extensions of ourselves. We only become individuals because we first learn to relate to other people and the world around us.

This enables us to develop a sense of identity and self-worth. We cannot exist on our own; therefore, objects as well as people become precious to us. Some would say that, at first, a baby does not see people, but objects. These objects are important and are incorporated into our world as we become emotionally and physically attached to them. The objects are not guaranteed to be with us forever, so we are vulnerable to the pain of separation and loss that are part of the process of growth and change. In marriage it is said that "the two become one flesh," although we retain our separate identities, we are also part of someone else and they of us.

To live and to love means accepting the inevitability of pain and loss. When we lose someone we love, it is called *bereavement* and the loss is experienced as grief. The pain of this grief cannot be cured by drugs. In fact it cannot be cured at all in the sense that some illnesses can be cured. For healing to begin, we have to experience the pain and allow it to be expressed.

As I've already emphasized, to cover up the pain or pretend it isn't there, to keep a stiff upper lip or see it as something you "get over," will only result in further and delayed suffering. We cannot bury the experience and the feelings associated with it and hope they will go away and not affect our lives. The experience stays there and requires energy to keep it repressed. In our unguarded moments, or when reminded of it by something or someone, it can come to the surface with a vengeance.

The Grieving Process

The process of grieving can be divided into four stages, although they are not fixed or rigidly defined. Some people will go through stages 1, 2, 3 and 4 in that order, while others might move from 1 to 3 and then back to 2 before reaching on to stage 4. Others seem to jump from one stage to another, and the feelings and reactions from different stages are all mixed up together.

However, it is convenient and useful to think of stages through which people can move. For one person, one stage might be long and drawn out, while for another it might be brief or nonexistent.

Sometimes the fourth stage is never reached and grieving continues at the same level without any apparent release or relief. This kind of grief is known as *complicated grief* and usually needs professional counseling or therapy to resolve. If grief is allowed expression, it seems to follow an identifiable pattern. There can be an initial shock, followed by a rise into anger and rage, and then a descent into the depths of depression. Gradually, if all goes well, there should be a slow ascent into healing, acceptance and peace.

Stage 1: Shock

> Mrs. Jones is sitting at home in the early evening expecting her husband to come home from work at any moment. Dinner is almost ready and she is reading the paper. Suddenly there is a knock on the door and a policeman asks if he can come in. Puzzled and a little frightened, she asks what it's about. He tells her that her husband has been killed in a car accident on his way home from work.

Her first reaction will probably be of shock. She might collapse and faint or run around screaming and shouting. This shock brings a sense of numbness and emptiness, as though something has suddenly been scraped out of her insides. In some ways, this feeling is a natural defense that enables the human mind and body to begin to cope with the unacceptable. It can continue for a long time and enable someone to go through the funeral, sort out the will, deal with insurance policies, pay the bills, deal with the money, car and all the other tasks. Often there are sensations of coldness, weakness and unreality.

Unreality and denial

Mrs. Jones's immediate reaction is to say

> You must have the wrong house. It can't be my husband.
> I saw him this morning before he left for work. His
> dinner is in the oven so it can't be him. Anyway, we are
> going to Hawaii for our vacation next week, so it must
> be another Mr. Jones.

All of these reactions of denial are part of the sense of unreality that the shock can bring. Some people become annoyed and angry with the one who brings the news and refuse to accept it. "He'll walk through the door at any moment. I hear his car right now."

Others experience very strongly the presence of the one who has died. This isn't surprising, not only because of the emotional and physical attachments, but also because the home will still contain constant reminders—his clothes are in the closets, the smell of his pipe lingers, photographs are there to bring back the memories and his slippers are still beside the bed. Even the dog or cat looks for his return every day. He's there and he isn't—this is part of the confusion that we struggle to come to terms with.

Similarly, in other traumatic incidents, there can be an initial reaction of shock and disbelief and the feeling that it isn't happening. This denial can even extend to thinking that it hasn't happened at all.

Crying

When they are bereaved, we expect the next-of-kin and relatives and friends to cry. This is the result of the shock and terrible feeling of sadness and loss.

> I can't stop crying. I don't know what to do. I lie in bed
> at night and know that he's not there. I miss him so
> much. The tears just won't stop, and I feel so stupid in
> front of other people. But I'll never see him again.

Sometimes people cannot stop crying. It goes on and on and pours out for no apparent reason. You can be sitting reading or watching the TV, when suddenly a terrible feeling of sadness overwhelms you, and you begin to cry. Others who don't know what to do or say can share this feeling of embarrassment. Helpers and carers can also share in the grief.

> Paul killed himself when his life fell apart. His wife, Joan, and their three children were away and found his body when they returned. The minister, a personal friend, traveled by car to see Paul's wife and on the way worked out very carefully what he would say. He rehearsed it almost word for word. When he arrived, Joan asked him in and they went into the living room and sat together on the sofa. He opened his mouth to speak and suddenly burst into tears. She put her arm around his shoulder to comfort him. It was also a tragic loss for him.

Crying is a natural way of relieving tension, sadness and pain and for most people is essential in the process of grieving. However, some are unable to cry. This may cause them more pain and guilt.

> I should be crying but I just can't. I did love him so much, but the tears won't come. I feel so empty and dried-up inside that there's no room for tears.

It may be that the tears come at the funeral, in church or at the graveside, but they might not come at all. It can be months or even years later when people break down and cry.

Shock, unreality, denial and sadness are normal reactions and can also be found in those who face the trauma of an accident or disaster or other losses in the process of normal living and growing. The fact is that post-trauma stress is a natural reaction to loss. As with bereavement, the initial response can be to erect an almost impenetrable barrier of denial in an attempt to avoid the flood of painful feelings and emotions.

Stage 2:Anger

> Mrs. Barber's son was killed in an accident at the factory.
> The funeral had been arranged and Mr. Green from the
> factory called to pay his respects. He told her how sorry
> he was but found it extremely difficult to know what to
> say. "I just called to say how sorry we all are about
> Robert . . ." And that's as far as he got.
>
> Mrs. Barber started shouting, "I know it's not your
> fault, but why did it happen to me? He's my only son.
> I've got nobody else but his father. Look at all the other
> young people who waste their lives on drinking and
> drugs. They're always in trouble. Robert never did a bad
> thing in his life. Why him? Why me? Anyway, why did
> you let him go into that place alone? He shouldn't have
> been there at all, the fool. He sometimes did such stupid
> things. And what about the doctor? Surely he could have
> saved Robert if he'd gotten there on time. They just can't
> be bothered. If he had been there sooner, Robert might
> still be alive."

The minister and her own doctor got the same treatment.
Anger can burst out suddenly and be directed at anybody who
happens to be available, especially if they can be blamed in any
way. There must be someone to blame. Other people laughing and
enjoying life, or just living, can
cause extreme outbursts of anger
and resentment.

Other people laughing and enjoying life, or just living, can cause extreme outbursts of anger and resentment.

Such anger can be very
distressing and embarrassing but, if
possible, should not be left bottled
up inside. It should be allowed expression and accepted by others
as normal, without any attempts to defend the person or
organization at which the anger is directed. Sometimes anger is
projected internally and is directed at self. Anger is common
following accidents, disasters and other traumatic events. It may be
directed at other victims, helpers and rescuers, bystanders and
organizations, and also at self.

Anger can be very disturbing, especially for those who believe
that feeling anger is wrong and should not be expressed, even

when it is felt. Men, especially, have difficulty handling their emotions and will attempt to contain the anger and keep it under control. This might be right for rescue workers who have to keep doing their job during the incident, but there should be an opportunity at a later stage for them to express what they feel.

Blame

When someone close to us dies, we need to find a reason and usually want to know "Why?" This is sometimes a practical question, but also, almost always, a question about meaning and purpose. It seems to be a natural part of the process if we can find something or someone to blame. Like anger, blame can be directed at anyone or everyone. This is sometimes the people who are seen to be responsible. The police for not preventing it, the doctor for not saving enough lives and God, who is a convenient scapegoat for just about everything else. In bereavement, blame can be directed at the person who has died, and in other traumatic incidents it can be fellow victims, even strangers, who are the focus. "How could they go and die like that? It's ruined my life and it's their fault. It makes me so angry. Why couldn't they have prevented it?"

This questioning can lead from anger and blame to the natural response of guilt. You can feel guilty for feeling guilty, or guilty for not feeling guilty! There can also be feelings of bitterness, regret and fear. Suddenly and sometimes violently, your life has changed and everything seems outside your control. You are vulnerable and frail in the face of what seems to be a hostile world.

Wanting to know "Why?" raises what can be called *ultimate questions*. "Why did it happen?" means more than wanting a practical answer. It is a cry of pain from the depths of anger and despair. No practical, trite or simple answer will suffice. Such answers can cause even deeper reactions and resentment.

In the many disasters of recent years questions have been asked about why the incidents happened. Anger and blame have been very much part of the response, both from individuals and from groups set up to help survivors and relatives. The desire for retribution has been seen by some as mercenary and the result of greed. But, like anger, blame is a natural and normal response to trauma and stress.

Investigations and inquests are often inconclusive or incomplete or not satisfactory. This has meant that for many, anger and blame have been intensified and become extremely important issues.

Placing blame is not simply a cry for vengeance, but a result of the desire and need for justice in what is experienced as an unjust world. Following some recent major disasters, it has seemed impossible to find answers to the questions survivors and relatives have asked. Investigations and inquests are often inconclusive or incomplete and have not been satisfactory. This has meant that for many, anger and blame have been intensified and become extremely important issues.

Longing and searching

This has been described as a burning ache deep inside for the person who has died, an ache that almost seems to explode. It is not uncommon for someone to be found walking the streets looking for their loved one. A woman who has lost a child may look at every baby stroller in the faint hope that she will see her baby, while a husband thinks that he sees his

Placing blame is not simply a cry for vengeance, but a result of the desire and need for justice in what is experienced as an unjust world.

dead wife in the supermarket. Someone with the same build or hairstyle, or with a familiar walk, can bring the instant hope that it is them. No sooner does the hope spring up inside, than it is dashed because we know that it cannot be true.

The desire to find and identify with the dead can be very strong when the body has not been recovered or was destroyed through war, an explosion, air crash or fire, or when people have been drowned, lost at sea or simply disappeared. There is nothing to see and seemingly nothing to grieve over.

The tragedy has happened but there is nothing on which the grief can be grounded and nowhere to focus it. This can increase the desire to find the person who has been lost.

When there is a body and it has been burned or mutilated in some way, it is often suggested that relatives should not see the body and they might be told to "remember him as he was."

> Catherine's son was killed in a car crash and she was advised not to see the body. It was there in the coffin, but she didn't see him. Her fears and fantasies grew and although she went through the funeral and burial, she had little with which to identify. Afterward, she said over and over again, "I should have seen him. He was my son. I wanted to see what he looked like just one more time, even if he looked awful. I would feel better if I had seen only his little finger." His clothes and belongings were put into the attic and nobody was allowed to touch them. Catherine believed that she had a right to see her son, but everyone prevented this and blocked every attempt she made. This made her grieving more difficult.

If Catherine had seen her son's body, it is probable that it would have helped her to come to terms with his death sooner. She constantly expected him to walk into the house and listened for the usual telephone call every Friday evening. The problem is that we think they can't be nowhere, they must be somewhere. And this can lead to a search for answers from religion.

"Surely death can't be the end?" Some will look for solace from a medium or spiritualist, while others will go over memories and try to relive the past. Photographs, videos and cassette tapes can bring back vivid memories of people, which can sometimes be satisfying and helpful, but at other times distressing and disturbing. People may have totally opposite reactions—some will destroy or get rid of everything that brings back memories, while others hoard it and store it.

Often people will send things to the Salvation Army or other charities, but keep other little items as reminders. There can never be any substitute for the person who has been lost, and nothing and no one can fill the aching void that is left behind. A similar response can be found in post-trauma stress reactions, in which there can be the desire to find and identify with other victims or to visit the graves of those killed in the incident.

Some may return to the site of the disaster in the hope that it will ease the burden and provide a solution to the deep longing and ache that is felt inside. After the Falklands War, the bodies of some servicemen killed there were brought home at the request of relatives. The normal British practice is to bury them in the country where they die. Later, relatives of those buried in the Falklands were given the opportunity to visit the graves.

One mother said that as they approached the shore in a boat, she expected to see her son standing there waiting to meet her. Even though she saw the grave, and this helped a little, she still expected to see her son. Often, relatives of the dead and survivors of accidents or disasters will say that a day never passes without some of the memories coming back. Longing and searching are common symptoms both of grief and of post-trauma stress.

Anxiety and fear

If my life has been threatened, and especially if I thought I was going to die, it is normal to be afraid and to feel that the same thing might happen again. Also, fear does not simply disappear once it has been experienced. It is persistent and can seem to have an its own existence. It's like an evil, black cloud or monster hovering around inside and out, waiting to engulf us and swallow us whole. This fear and anxiety can seldom be kept at bay and is summed up in this saying by an anonymous author: "No man can hide from his own fears, for they are part of him and they will always know where he is hiding."

This fear and anxiety can be tied in with re-experiencing, avoidance and arousal, characteristic symptoms of post-trauma stress discussed in chapter 3. The anxiety can emerge as confusion and panic. Will it happen again? Will the feelings ever go away? Why am I so frightened and anxious? Am I ill? What am I going to do now? How will I live? Who will look after me? Will I have to sell the house and move? What about the funeral? Will I cope? How can I go on? Will I ever be normal again? The symptoms of fear can be experienced as physical sensations. C. S. Lewis, after his wife's death, wrote in *A Grief Observed,*

> No one ever told me that grief felt so like fear . . . the same fluttering in the stomach, the same restlessness, the yawning. I kept swallowing . . .

If you are involved in an accident or disaster, it would be abnormal if you did not experience anxiety or fear at some level. All of these reactions—anger, the need to blame, guilt, bitterness, regret, longing and searching, anxiety and fear—are normal and natural reactions to loss, bereavement and the trauma of accidents or disasters.

Stage 3: Depression

A descent into depression is common in grief, or following any traumatic incident, and it includes feelings of helplessness, loneliness, self-reproach, loss of identity and isolation. The initial shock and the sense of unreality and numbness can be followed by extreme anger and, in bereavement, the clinging desire not to let go of the one who has gone. This heightened sense of activity can then descend into the depths of depression.

> What's the point? He's gone, and I just can't seem to cope any more or be bothered about anything. People still come to see me, but what's the use? I don't really want to see anybody. Anyway, they just don't understand how I feel. They can't, can they, unless it's happened to them? The pain seems to get worse every day. I thought I'd be feeling better by now and people told me I'd get over it in time. But it's useless trying any more. The pain and hurt just go on and on.

The same reactions can be found in accident or disaster victims and the condition can last for many months or years. We've all known a widow who hides in the past, grieving over her husband until the day she dies. Life seems to slow down and become meaningless. Those who try to care—clergy, doctors, relatives and friends, social workers and volunteers—feel they are facing an impenetrable barrier of depression and apathy, and those at the center feel that it will never end.

Isolation and loss of self identity and self-worth

The experience of external loss is reflected internally through feelings of isolation and a reduced sense of self-worth or value. A disaster or accident victim, or the relative of someone killed, may feel useless, impotent and helpless.

> Before the accident I felt I was somebody. I was good at my job. Now I've lost all confidence in myself. People avoid me at work, and when I speak to them they say they don't want to hear about the crash. I feel so awful and alone that I could scream, but I just retreat into myself. I suppose I'm an embarrassment to them. People try to be kind, but what do they really know or care? It didn't happen to them. I feel so lonely and isolated and don't seem to know who I am any more. I feel so useless and helpless.

Loss of faith and purpose

Following an accident in which her husband was killed, a woman who survived with her children said

> The minister called the other day and told me that I should be grateful that I've got the children to look after me and to remind me of John. He said that God is good, but he doesn't know what it's like for me. If God is good, why does He allow such dreadful things to happen? Life is so unfair. But why bother and what does it all matter anyway? Everything is a waste of time and of life. If there is a God, and He does things like this, then I don't want to know Him.

Some will lose faith and others find it. When someone you love has died, or when you are involved in trauma, the initial shock means that you are in no condition to begin to think things through logically or sensibly. Sweet words of comfort can be meaningless.

Some people lose a sense of purpose, while others throw themselves into volunteer work and look for some kind of satisfaction in helping other people. Some believe that there is no purpose in life because their entire world has fallen apart and everything seems like a complete waste of time.

Loneliness

Bereavement and loss seem to carry a stigma.

> After the accident, many people didn't know what to
> do or say when they met me. People don't mean to be
> unkind, but often they don't know what to say or do to
> help, and the easiest course of action is either to stay away
> and ignore you or never mention it. Some even cross the
> street or hide to avoid contact or having to speak.

Often the fear is that something will "rub off" or that disaster
and tragedy are "catching." This only serves to make the feeling of
being alone more intense.

Once the traumatic incident is over, there can be a sense of abandonment and feeling that nobody cares.

In bereavement, this loneliness can be further confirmed when the funeral is over and family and friends have left. For victims of accidents and disasters, it can happen when they return home. The hustle and turmoil of the incident and involvement of the media all make for a high profile at the time and shortly after, but once the traumatic incident is over there can be a sense of abandonment and feeling that nobody cares. Relatives, neighbors and friends can be involved and give support for a short while, but they have their own lives to lead and their interest tends to wane. Their expectation is that in a short time you will be all right and back to normal. It is easy for others to lose patience. Being with those who are suffering trauma and loss requires a great deal of effort and energy.

It is easy for others to lose patience. Being with those who are suffering trauma and loss requires a great deal of effort and energy.

Some suggest that you must make drastic changes in your life— move to a new house or apartment, take a vacation, or go and stay with well-meaning friends or family. Sometimes these are the worst things you can do, for this only causes more change and loss. Support is important, but it is also necessary to try and retain whatever sense of dignity and independence is left.

Physical Loss

A close relationship normally means physical closeness and sex, and when the other person dies, all this is gone. It has already been said that trauma often triggers either clinging and a need for love and affection, or a complete rejection of any physical contact. Either reaction can cause problems. Some people tend to lose sympathy as they get on with their lives. Being avoided and denied physical contact can be very hurtful and there may be a deep sense of physical and sexual deprivation.

> I can smell his presence in the house and feel that he is still here. I know he's gone, but everything around me reminds me of him. I lie in the single bed in the spare room because our own room holds too many memories. I couldn't sleep in the double bed without him, it feels so empty at night. I so much want to be held and loved by him, but he's not here to comfort me.

Occasionally, some find comfort and solace with other people and sometime at a very early stage in the grief.

> Allan was 72 when his wife died in an accident, and he then lived on his own for a while. Through a local organization he met Judy, age 26, and discovered that they had a mutual interest in photography. Within a short time she moved in with him, much to the anger and frustration of his family and friends. Judy was an unwanted intrusion into their own grief and loss and some described him as a "dirty old man." They didn't understand what he was doing or why.

Physical contact is usually very important and if you don't feel able to hug someone, just a touch on the hand or arm can be sufficient. However, some will not want to be touched or held and can seem cold and distant.

This stage of depression following trauma can last for a long time. Some become trapped in their feelings of isolation and loneliness. It is as though they have descended into a pit from which they cannot escape. Their feeling is that there is no God, nobody cares and all is without meaning or purpose.

Stage 4: Acceptance and Healing

Many seem to think that grief and the reactions of post-trauma stress are relatively short-term problems that go away pretty quickly if you are determined to get on with your life and not moan or complain. Again we hear the response, "You'll get over it soon." The belief that you will "get over it" is partly a defense against having to be involved too deeply. It is also a protection from thinking about what it would mean if it happened to you.

> *Unfortunately, you do not "get over" grief or post-trauma stress, you only go into it—and either stay there or go through it.*

Unfortunately, you do not "get over" grief or post-trauma stress, you only go into it—and either stay there or go through it.

Perhaps the most difficult thing to realize about this stage is that the pain experienced contains within it the seeds of healing and renewal. Normal grief and stress reactions are not signs of an illness or sickness that needs medication or psychiatric help. Losing means pain. The result of that pain is shock, anger and depression, and the many other complex feelings and reactions that loss brings into our lives. To dismiss death or a traumatic incident as trivial or unimportant suggests either that we don't care or are defending ourselves against the unbearable pain that we know is there inside.

The truth is that if we are allowed to express the pain, no matter how difficult or distressing it might be, we usually begin to cope and learn to value our lives and selves again. The pain should be "gone through," not "gotten over," because if we think that we have gotten over it, we will find that the terrible pain and feelings of loss remain locked inside, eating away at us like a cancer and preventing us from healing and attaining peace. If the pain is experienced, we can eventually come to terms with it and learn that even at its worst it cannot destroy us. We can survive and go on.

This does not mean that the pain disappears. The feelings are still inside, but we recognize them as signs that we do care about what has happened. We are responding and reacting in a normal way to the experience. Hopefully a new sense of well-being emerges and we learn to love life once more. Yet it can be more than this, for some achieve a deeper sense of peace and acceptance and feel that they have grown in maturity, strength and confidence.

Many who have survived accidents and disasters will say that when they were able to work through their experiences they emerged much more capable and self-assured. They know that they have survived. Although they didn't believe that it would ever happen, they have a new sense of their own worth and value. This can also be true of grief.

As time passes, identification with the one we have lost can become stronger than ever. In her book *Death and the Family,* Lily Pincus describes how, many years after her husband's death, she began to feel a stronger sense of his presence, which increased as

> *Many who have survived accidents and disasters will say that when they were able to work through their experiences, they emerged much more capable and self-assured.*

time went by. Her husband became more a part of her than ever before: "Only when the lost person has been internalized and become part of the bereaved . . . is the mourning process complete." She felt a deep sense of peace and that life was more important than ever before. This experience does not happen to everyone, but most people seem to learn to cope and carry on with their lives. They move through a host of deeply disturbing emotions and feelings and yet still feel that their lives are worth living. They can find new interests, new partners and friends, and new hope.

Summary

I've already emphasized that there are losses in life other than bereavement, accidents or disasters that can also be traumatic and result in post-trauma stress. These include

- Moving
- Long periods of separation from family
- Going into or coming out of the hospital or prison
- Having a vasectomy, hysterectomy, losing a limb or any similar operation involving loss and change
- Going to day or boarding school
- Losing or leaving a job

- Experiencing violence—robbery, war, murder, suicide, rape

- Destruction of buildings and environment

- Physical threat to self, family or friends

Grieving and learning to cope with trauma is normally a long-term process. It is never the same for any two people. It can divide families and couples as well as bring them together, and it can last for years. There is no easy solution except to remember that it is normal and that it takes time. In the case of bereavement, some will say that after a year they are just beginning to see their way through it, while others find that after a year the pain is worse.

However, the trauma and loss of bereavement and the experience of being involved in an accident or disaster lasts a lifetime and becomes part of our hidden agenda. It can be rather like the sea on the shore. Sometimes it surges up into our consciousness like a great wave breaking on the rocks, and at other times it seems to appear as a memory from the past, like the gentle flow of the surf over the sand.

The event, and the feelings, sensations and emotions associated with the experience, are still there, buried deep in our minds. Months or years later, a sight, sound, smell or touch can bring the memories flooding back. The pain can still be there, but if we have been able to face the emotions and feelings and express them, we will have learned to move on in our lives. The good as well as the painful memories remain, but we have incorporated them into our life experiences. Although they may surface occasionally, we know that they are normal and cannot destroy us; we can survive, cope and continue with our lives.

Further Reading

Bowlby, John. *Attachment*. New York: Basic Books, 1983.

—*The Making & Breaking of Affectional Bonds*. New York: Routledge, 1979.

Erikson, Erik H. *Childhood & Society*. New York: W.W. Norton & Company, Inc., 1993

Rogers, Carl. *On Becoming a Person*. Houghton Mifflin Company, 1972.

Skynner, Robin, and John Cleese. *Families & How to Survive Them*. London and New York: Oxford University Press, Inc., 1985.

6

Coping

CERTAIN ATTITUDES AND BELIEFS of the society we live in can make it more difficult for us to cope with loss, whether from bereavement, post-trauma stress or any of the other losses we experience in life.

In part, these are due to the many changes that have taken place in our recent history and culture. They include denial, a common attitude toward any kind of post-trauma stress or loss, lack of contact with the experience of loss and reduction in social support. For some, there may be the use of rituals and, for many, the opposite: loss of any formal religious beliefs.

Denial of the Reality

It is common to deny that such a thing as post-trauma stress exists. We pretend it doesn't exist and suggest that it only affects those who are weak or lacking in moral, mental or physical strength.

If you have been brought up to believe that you should face problems with a certain toughness of body, mind and intellect, it becomes more difficult to cope with the trauma of an accident, disaster or death. "When the going gets tough, the tough get going." This is the bulldog attitude that smiles in the face of catastrophe and crisis. Unfortunately this does not work for most of us, because it involves pushing away the experiences to a spot deeply buried in our minds in the hope or belief that they will not touch or affect us.

The most common reaction to post-trauma stress and loss seems to be to deny that they exist. Like death, accidents happen to others, not to us, and we cope by pushing them aside or inside, and ignoring them. If we expect to have a tough attitude when faced with a crisis, when we do experience trauma and loss, our reactions may be far stronger than we are prepared to handle.

Lack of Contact with Loss and Trauma

It seems to be true that people in our society are generally healthier than ever before and, on average, we live longer than our ancestors did. Most people do not experience serious accidents or disasters in their lives, and death, until it comes to us, is fairly remote. Woody Allen, the comedian and director, summed up this attitude when he said, "I'm not afraid of dying. I just don't want to be there when it happens."

Our views on these very personal matters can easily become cold and clinical, and death and grief become more remote, partly due to the dispersal and disintegration of close family groups and ties. Children rarely see death close at hand as a normal part of life. They are often discouraged from attending funerals in an attempt to shield them from pain. Because many people move around so much and no longer live and die in the same area, old people tend not to live with or near children and their families.

Our culture has seen an increase in the number of homes and apartments created especially with built-in care for the elderly in mind. Although this might provide better care for them, it removes them from their immediate families and prevents their families from having close contact with them, with old age and with death.

The same can be said to some extent for the hospice movement. Although it brings many benefits, such as constant professional care, relief from pain, and counseling and support for the patient and family, there are also disadvantages. When hospice care is not provided in the home but in a dedicated facility, it can result in a loss of contact with old age and death. The hospice movement might not help us to cope with these realities because death becomes something to be kept in a special place rather than being a normal and natural event in life. This is far from the days when people, of whatever age, usually died at home among family and friends. The message today seems to be that death, and therefore loss and its associated feelings and emotions, are to be avoided if possible.

The belief seems to be that if we shelter people from pain, they won't feel or experience it. Pain and loss are to be seen as abnormal, and so are the feelings and reactions associated with them. This approach is not true of many other societies or communities, where death in particular is surrounded by encouragement to grieve. Some societies even include professional mourners who can be hired for the occasion. Also, death and disaster are more common in some countries than others. Earthquakes, tornadoes, hurricanes and other natural disasters are common in some parts of the world. Some people live every day with poverty, famine, disease and death as constant companions.

> *The belief seems to be that if we shelter people from pain, they won't feel or experience it.... This approach is not true of many other societies ... where death in particular is surrounded by encouragement to grieve.*

These hardships make the experiences of loss and trauma more common, but it does not mean that they are therefore more acceptable or less painful for those concerned. It is easy to think that because I experience disaster on a regular basis, the trauma will be easier to accept and therefore I will cope better. This is probably not true.

It may be that the post-trauma stresses are compounded and made worse rather than easier when disasters are more common in a person's life. When we look at the faces of starving people in the Third World, we do not see the faces of people who no longer care, but of those who have almost certainly retreated into numbness and a severe form of depression, helplessness and loss of purpose. These are typical symptoms of grief, loss and post-trauma stress, although the post-trauma stress experienced in this case is ongoing.

Reduced Social Support

When communities were closer together and smaller, it was common for individuals and families suffering trauma or loss to be supported by large sections of the community. This is certainly less true because of the move from small-town communities to large towns, cities and suburbs. In such living conditions there is little or no personal contact, and for many there is less support in times of need.

> Mary lived for eight years in an apartment in a new suburb on the outskirts of Chicago, but had been brought up in the city and lived there until her husband retired. When her husband died, she had no family to call upon other than a son who had moved to New York with his family. She had no other relatives or friends. After the funeral her son returned to New York, and she was left to grieve alone. She lived on the eighth floor, and the elevator was almost always broken. She did not know any of her neighbors, who worked and only came home in the late evening. She was surrounded by people, but this only seemed to increase her feelings of loneliness and isolation. Within a year she died, some said from a broken heart, but to her it seemed that nobody cared and there was nothing to live for any more.

A lack of family and community support further magnifies the stigma associated with death and loss. Our upbringing and social conditioning can imply that it is best to avoid death and loss if possible. If I have no experience with trauma and I get the strong message to avoid it, then it will be more difficult for me to face and cope with trauma. However, like it or not, loss and trauma are basic to our experiences in life.

Part of the conflict is that we have experienced losses in our life previously and have learned various coping methods, some of which are more helpful than others. But other people tell us to be strong and not show feelings or express them. These mixed messages tell us that our contact with grief and trauma should be minimal—and avoided entirely if possible.

Absence of Rituals
This applies especially to death and the process of grief, but it also has significance for post-trauma-stress reactions. Rituals surround the major events in our lives, from birth and marriage to death, but

in recent years there has been a tendency to minimize them. We are all very busy in our lives, especially when it comes to the pain of tragedy. We can easily attempt to avoid any contact or involvement with the experience by staying busy with other important parts of our lives.

Rituals can threaten us because they remind us that death and disaster are always nearby. Some people may adopt an attitude that says basically, "Keep the rituals short because we do not want to cause further pain."

In a situation involving a death, how can anyone cause someone who is grieving more pain than already exists? If my wife has died, or I have been involved in an accident, then the pain is there, even if it is repressed and denied. Reminding me about it or talking about my wife probably will cause pain, but this is not new pain. It comes from deep within and is already there, inside. It must come out, it must be expressed. Sometimes the desire to avoid pain is more for the benefit of those around the person who is grieving than for the person who is primarily affected.

At a seminar to prepare carers for coping with casualties following a disaster, someone asked whether the doctor should be asked to give victims and survivors medication to calm them down. A psychiatrist stood up and said, "If the doctor is called, tranquilizers should be reserved for the spectators, to calm *them* down. [Carers] should sit with the casualty, hold their hand, give them comfort and, if appropriate, encourage them to talk."

The question to ask is, whose pain are we trying to avoid by minimizing rituals—the victim's pain or our own? Rituals are a necessary part of the grieving process, because they enable people to focus their emotions, acknowledge the death, give permission for mourning to begin or continue, provide social, family and community support and give dignity to the dead. Rituals also provide an opportunity not only for expressing grief, but also for showing respect and giving thanks for the lives of those who have died.

There is no doubt that the rituals and ceremonies following a disaster are of inestimable benefit not only for survivors and relatives, but also for carers and helpers. It is also beneficial for those who watch the disaster scenes on television and are deeply disturbed; they need to focus their feelings and emotions and feel a sense of solidarity with those who are grieving.

Loss of Belief

Church attendance in our society is in decline, and so is the number of people who definitely commit themselves to any particular belief. Although most people still say they believe in God, a survey some years ago showed that of those who go to church regularly, less than 50% believed in any kind of life after death. Those who have a deep and profound faith, whether in an orthodox religion or atheism and humanism, can be helped by their beliefs to cope with grief and trauma, but it does not mean that they will not grieve.

> Richard was a devout evangelical Christian who believed that everything that happened had a purpose and was part of God's greater plan. Before his wife died after being involved with him in an accident, he stayed by her side every day throughout the many weeks she spent in a coma in the hospital. He believed in the power of prayer and prayed hard for her to be healed. When she died, he tried to remain strong and told himself that he must thank God for her life and that it was wrong to grieve because she was now with her Father. Unfortunately this strategy didn't work for Richard.
>
> After the funeral, he was totally overwhelmed by an all-consuming grief that completely shattered his faith. He felt guilty at having survived. He thought that he was partly responsible for the accident, and that he had failed himself, his wife and, above all, the Church and God. He felt angry with God, and descended into a depression; he felt life was a waste of time and without purpose. Richard was going through the process of grief and post-trauma stress and didn't know it. Facing his dying wife each day had drained him physically, mentally and spiritually and trying to remain strong had only made matters worse.
>
> His Christian friends tried to help, but told him that he must pray and remember that his wife had died

because it was God's will. Others said that if he had
prayed harder, she might have been healed, so perhaps
he lacked faith. A few more "devout" Church members
even suggested that she had died as a kind of
punishment by God because of something either he or
she had done wrong. It was a punishment for sin and he
must look into his past life and seek forgiveness.

Little wonder that he lost his faith! It seems that he was
doomed to disaster from the beginning. The faith that had been so
important to him collapsed when his wife died. He believed that
he would not feel any grief, and he could have done without the
advice of those who claimed to be his friends.

Even so, those who do have a very strong faith and belong to
a supportive community, such
as a church or other
organization, seem to cope
better than those who do not.

> *Those who do have a very strong faith and belong to a supportive community, such as a church or other organization, seem to cope better than those who do not.*

Those who survived best
in concentration camps in
World War II were those who
had an inner faith and strength that came from religious or political
belief. Some have said that Christians, Muslims and Communists
survived better than others, and in his book, *The Informed Heart,*
Bruno Bettelheim states that Jehovah's Witnesses were among
those who coped best.

> Similar behavior (aloofness and emotional distance)
> characterized another group which, according to
> psychoanalytic theory, would have had to be viewed as
> extremely neurotic or plainly delusional, and therefore
> apt to fall apart, as persons, under post-trauma stress. I
> refer to Jehovah's Witnesses, who not only showed
> unusual heights of human dignity and moral behavior,
> but seemed protected against the same camp experience
> that soon destroyed persons considered well integrated
> by my psychoanalytic friends and myself.

Bettelheim adds that those who survived the concentration
camp were the ones who were able to retain their humanity amid
the degradation and horror.

Those prisoners who blocked out neither heart nor
reason, neither feelings nor perception, but kept
informed of their inner attitudes even when they could
hardly ever afford to act on them—those prisoners
survived and came to understand the conditions they
lived under. They also came to realize what they had not
perceived before; that they still retained the last, if not
the greatest, of human freedoms: to choose their own
attitudes in any given circumstance. Prisoners who
understood this fully came to know that this, and only
this, formed the crucial difference between retaining
one's humanity (and often life itself) and accepting death
as a human being.

A firm belief and conviction can help survival, but is not an
insurance policy or guarantee against suffering. Experiences of
bereavement and trauma can happen to anyone and the result is
loss, even if we deny it and bury it. To believe that you will meet
your loved ones again in heaven can give you immense strength
and comfort, but you still need to grieve. Jesus said that those who
mourn are blessed for they will be
comforted *(Matthew 5:4)* and
perhaps he meant that in order to
be blessed and comforted you
need to experience the pain, for
only those who do can hope to
find healing and peace. This is also true for any kind of trauma or
loss. To deny or try to avoid the feelings will almost certainly lead
to further and deeper difficulties.

> *A firm belief and conviction
> can help survival, but is not
> an insurance policy or
> guarantee against suffering.*

Here again we face the problem of belief when we consider
the male-dominated attitudes apparent in some sections of society.
It is the problem of the macho image of men, which involves the
belief that women should and can express emotions, but not
men—at least not "real" men. Under this belief, to express emotion
is a sign of weakness or lack of character. I have already
emphasized that this is a particular problem among members of
organizations such as the armed forces, the police, prison guards
and fire and rescue services.

> After a major air crash, male and female members of the
> army from a nearby camp were called in to help in the
> rescue and cleaning-up process. Some saw dead bodies
> and had to pick up body parts and personal belongings.
> Afterward, when they met to talk about their experiences,
> the women found it easy to talk, but the men stayed
> silent and kept their feelings to themselves. Few talked
> about it, even to their friends. The standard operating
> procedure seems to have been this: Soldiers should not
> cry or be upset, and certainly not in front of women!

A healthier approach is the belief that it is *all right* for men to cry and show emotion. This is not easy to do when you have been brought up to believe the opposite and to accept peer-group pressure, which tells you to be hard and tough in order to be a man. Men who are brought up with these values learn that if you are a man you must not cry or show emotion when you face tragedy, accidents or disaster, whether as a victim or a carer.

All of these minimizing values and beliefs present serious problems when we consider coping strategies for traumatic experiences and loss. Some internal and external supports that we used to rely upon are either gone or have been diminished—be they social, spiritual or physical. Post-trauma stress and loss reactions are seen as "unnecessary."

The way we think about trauma and loss determines our ability to cope with the feelings and emotions that are generated by these experiences. It determines the attitudes of those who suffer as victims and of those who try to help. If we are brought up to push our feelings aside and to treat sufferers as though they are ill or weak, we will be unable to face both their feelings and our own.

It's a healthy society that takes trauma and loss seriously and accepts as normal and natural the reactions of grief and post-trauma stress.

Coping with Trauma and Loss

Coping with minor stresses is a normal part of everyone's life. Traveling, telephone calls, letters, news, arguments, disappointments, anxieties and worries, problems with partners, children, neighbors, work and colleagues, are all stressful to some extent, but usually we learn to cope, even if some situations make us frustrated, angry and upset. Coping with deeply disturbing traumatic events may cause problems that are more difficult to deal with or accept.

Our ability to cope depends on a number of factors, such as personality and character, previous experiences, the traumatic extent of the event and the nature of the support we are given. But it must be clearly understood that most people will cope most of the time and be able to continue with their lives. Don't imagine or believe that post-trauma stress will always damage or destroy one's life, because some will suffer no symptoms whatsoever and remain cool, calm and collected throughout and after the incident.

> *Most people will cope most of the time and be able to continue with their lives.*

As I've stated previously, external reactions, or lack of them, *do not necessarily* indicate that a person is coping adequately. Nevertheless, some people do cope very well and claim to emerge as even stronger people, with better personal relationships and marriages and a greater ability to cope in the future. The positive side of this is that involvement in a disaster can make people more aware of the importance of life and of human relationships. For some people, it can help create a strong belief in the value and purpose of life.

Human beings have an extraordinary capacity to cope under extremely difficult conditions and events, as we have seen in hostages released from captivity in the Middle East. They were living a life that for them was normal, and then they were taken hostage, enduring extreme physical and mental deprivation for years through isolation, fear, hunger, threat, torture and intimidation.

> *Human beings have an extraordinary capacity to cope under extremely difficult conditions and events.*

On their release, no matter how relieved they were to be free, they had to come to terms with the trauma of returning to their own countries, families and friends—returning to what must have seemed by then an alien and foreign world. Their task was, and is, to adjust to being back in a world that developed and changed in their absence.

The same challenge applies to service personnel returning from the many wars of the past 100 years, including the Gulf War and Somalia. It applies to those involved in accidents and disasters as victims or helpers, to their families and friends and others in a much wider circle of support and contact. Anyone touched by a disaster or trauma, however peripherally, needs to learn how to cope, not only with survivors and others, but also with their own feelings and reactions to the experience.

> *Anyone touched by a disaster or trauma, however peripherally, needs to learn how to cope, not only with survivors and others, but also with their own feelings and reactions to the experience.*

The most important things to remember about trauma and loss are

- They are natural and normal reactions.

- They should be allowed expression.

- They involve a long-term process.

The Normality of Reactions

Post-traumatic-stress reactions, like those of grief, are completely natural and normal. They can be overwhelming in their intensity sometimes, but even this is not necessarily abnormal. Some problems need professional help and counseling to resolve, especially in the case of *complicated grief* or *post-traumatic stress disorder*, in which victims are trapped in a particular stage or state and are unable to work through their feelings. It also depends on the nature of the traumatic event, especially when the experience is terrifying or life threatening. Post-traumatic-stress reactions may be connected with inappropriate or inadequate patterns of behavior learned earlier in life as strategies for coping with problematic situations.

> Christopher had been brought up by his father to believe that "men don't cry." When his pet rabbit died he felt terrible, but because he was frightened of his father, he didn't let himself cry. When he was 11, his grandmother died and he was devastated. Again, his father told him he shouldn't cry and threatened to beat him if he did.

Christopher's constant experience was that he belonged to a family where feelings were denied. He coped with grief and emotion by denying it and burying it inside. When he was involved with his wife in an accident, he found that he couldn't understand his wife's outbursts of emotion and was unable to cope with her nightmares and eventual depression. Gradually they drifted apart and lived separate lives. He was trapped in an emotional ice block of denial.

Little wonder that Christopher could not begin to cope except by retreating into himself and denying the need to grieve. Those who are trying to help can feel that they are being engulfed, not only by the intensity of the feelings of victims and others, but by their own emotions and reactions. They retreat or become irritated and unsympathetic in an attempt to protect themselves.

Expressing Feelings and Emotions

A fairly common attitude is that you get over grief and trauma within a few months at the most, after which you'll be back to normal. This is untrue. The fact is that something *has* happened to you, and even though you might defend yourself against what happened with behaviors and attitudes of denial, the experience remains part of you. Eventually it will express itself one way or another.

It might be denial, silence, withdrawal and a total numbness, which others interpret as strength, or uncontrolled outbursts of anger and violence. It's especially true if feelings are repressed. It can be expressed through various nonspecific illnesses, including chest pains, depression, listlessness, headaches, stomach troubles and absence from work or difficulties in relationships.

A Long-Term Process

The experience of post-trauma stress, like that of grief, stays with us for the rest of our lives and becomes incorporated into our inner world. Even if the pain and memories have faded, they are still buried and can emerge later as a dull ache inside or as deep feelings of regret and sadness. The symptoms can return or be expressed later and be much more disturbing.

> I thought I had coped with it, but the old feelings
> occasionally come back and sometimes I think that I will
> never learn to accept them. It's very frightening, not only
> to experience them again, but also to know that they are
> still hanging around inside, waiting to break out. When
> they do, I almost feel that they are going to engulf me.

How long does this last? The answer is that there is no set period of time, only the knowledge that the experience will remain with us for the rest of our lives. With post-trauma stress, many people cope well at the time or within a matter of days, but some will live with symptoms for periods ranging from a few weeks to months or years.

If symptoms persist or recur for more than a month and are disturbing or disabling, post traumatic stress disorder may be diagnosed. How one reacts depends on a number of factors already mentioned—the coping mechanisms of the individual, the nature of the event and the support given at the time and later.

People are less likely to cope if

- The incident is particularly traumatic or life threatening.

- The individual has poor coping strategies and inner resources or a history of mental problems.

- There is lack of support during the incident and shortly after.

- Little or no help, counseling or debriefing is offered later.

As noted earlier, it is impossible to say how anyone will cope, either at the time or later. Someone who appears to be coping might be suffering in silence. Another person who is crying or screaming might recover quickly. In bereavement, it is said that it takes an average of about two years to achieve healing, but some will feel a sense of recovery earlier and some much later.

A few will remain stuck with their feelings until the day they die. If we are given support through psychological debriefing and if we can work through the feelings and emotional reactions, we will grow into a period when we feel that we are attaining some kind of peace and acceptance. Life begins to look good again. We make new relationships and move ahead with confidence; but the feelings have not disappeared.

> When her mother died in an accident, Katherine went
> through the process of grieving quite well. Four years
> later, she was walking in a shopping mail when suddenly
> she began to cry. Her husband took her arm and asked
> what was wrong. She said that she had seen a woman
> with the same hairstyle and build as her mother and the
> memories had come flooding back. Although she had
> coped with her grief, the feelings were there under the
> surface years later.

A clear understanding of the grief process and the nature of post-trauma-stress reactions will help all who are involved in traumatic incidents, including victims. This understanding is necessary, not only for professional helpers such as clergy, doctors and medical staff, but also for members of the police, fire and rescue services and the armed forces. It also applies to supporting agencies such as the social services and other helping and counseling organizations.

Methods and Strategies for Coping and Helping

The strategies for helping and coping suggested here are useful to everyone and anyone involved during and after a traumatic incident, from victims and rescuers to families, friends and helpers in an ever-widening circle.

The main methods of helping are similar to the ways people are enabled to cope with other kinds of loss. This is by encouraging them to express their feelings, work through them and eventually discover the strength and purpose to continue with their lives. The following was written by Brian Eageran in an article in the newspaper *The Guardian* on August 9, 1991, shortly after the release of his friend and fellow hostage John McCarthy. It reflects the words of Bruno Bettelheim quoted earlier.

> Each man must find within himself the various methods
> to contain and control the pain and confusion within.
> There are no ready-made answers. It is a slow process of
> rediscovery, where denial or flight from the inward
> turmoil is the antithesis of self-healing. We go that road

> alone. We may be helped, but we cannot be pushed or
> misdirected. We each have the power within us to
> rehumanize ourselves. We are our own self-healers.

This says quite clearly that the aftereffects of a traumatic
experience need to be dealt with, but that the power to heal must
come from within. Others can help and give support, but it is the
individual who must face the situation, discover his or her own inner
resources and find the strength to go on. Denial and retreat from the
feelings only make things worse and
may cause further trauma.

The power to heal must come from within.

Ultimately, healing can come only
from the inside and in the struggle to
remain human. The strategies and methods suggested are not the
same as psychological debriefing, which will be discussed in
chapter 8, although they are part of the same process of helping
and debriefers should be aware of them. We are brought up in a
society that persuades us to deny the reality of death and hide our
feelings, but in fact the way to cope with trauma and loss is to do
exactly the opposite.

There are four main tasks:

1. To help people to accept the reality of their experiences
   and to counteract the defense of denial.

2. To encourage them to feel the pain and to provide
   reassurance of the normality of their reactions. This also
   deals with the problem of denial.

3. To help them adjust and adapt to the changes that have
   taken place in their lives.

4. To help them redirect their emotions and their lives so
   they can move to acceptance and healing.

Accepting the Reality of the Experience
Here we try to counteract the problem of denial.

Being specific about the incident
The first aim is to help people face the fact that they have been
involved in an accident or disaster. If people have been killed or

seriously injured—strangers, relatives, friends or colleagues—this should be talked about openly. If it is a death, then be specific about the death without using flowery words or phrases. Avoid using expressions such as "passed away," "deceased," "gone away" or "been taken from us."

Be direct and use the words *death, dead, died* and *killed*. "I'm very sorry to hear about Mary's death. It must be terrible for you." The problem is that if the experience is not talked about or the death is denied as a fact, then soft words may prevent the other people involved from facing the stark reality of what has happened to them. You can be precise without being brutal.

Soft words may prevent the other people involved from facing the stark reality of what has happened to them.

Sometimes people who have survived a traumatic event will try to pretend that the accident was not serious and that they are all right, or that the person who died is not dead. Even years after a traumatic incident, some people will not be able to talk about it and will try to keep up the pretense that all is well. In extreme cases, some will deny that the event happened at all.

Coping with the Body

Viewing the body

In the case of a death in an accident or disaster, if it is possible, encourage relatives and survivors to see the body. Some will not want to, but they should be gently and sensitively encouraged to do so. No matter how distressing the experience, viewing the body should help them to accept that the incident has happened and that the person is dead. They can see it for themselves. Also, it is an occasion when they can pay their respects, acknowledge the person as the one who is known and loved and, if it is their practice, to say some prayers.

> Debbie was seven when she was killed playing on a jungle gym, which fell over and crushed her. Her body was taken to the local hospital and laid out in a small room. Her parents, Brian and Helen, asked the chaplain if they should see her, and the chaplain suggested that it

would help them if they could do so. Helen was very
reluctant, but eventually agreed, and the chaplain went
with them into the room.

They cried, comforted each other, stood in silence
for a few minutes, and then asked the chaplain to say a
prayer. Shortly after the funeral, Brian and Helen had to
move to another town because of Brian's work, and the
chaplain received a letter from them saying that they
were grateful they had seen Debbie before the funeral
because they knew that if they hadn't, they would have
regretted it later. It had helped them to accept her death
and to grieve.

Although, in the end, their feelings and wishes should be
respected, relatives should be encouraged to see the body, even if
it is badly disfigured or damaged. It has been said that often the
reality isn't as bad as the fantasies that can develop, either at the
time or later. Even if it is as bad, or worse, it confirms the reality of
the death and helps to prevent denial.

Absence of a body

People need contact with the dead to help them identify with their
loved ones and accept what has happened. Viewing a body is
possible when there is a body, but visiting may be discouraged
because there has been a death in an airplane crash, a traffic accident or other disaster in which the body has been badly disfigured,
mutilated or is decomposed or incomplete.

It may seem macabre to some, but many relatives say that they
would like to see the body, or even part of it, no matter what
condition it is in. It is important to them to have something, or
literally some body, with which they can identify.

Sara's husband was killed in an helicopter crash and she
had asked to see his body, but was refused on the
grounds that it was in a bad state and it would only
cause her pain. She asked to see a photograph of the
body and was refused again for the same reasons.
Finally, she asked to see where his body had been
found, but was told that this was not possible. She was
extremely angry and said over and over again, "He was

my husband. I had the right to see him, or even part of
him. If I could just have seen something of him it would
have helped me to accept that he had died."

Visiting the scene of the incident

In the case of accidents or disasters, some may wish to visit the
place where it happened. This is not absolutely necessary, but
some will insist on doing so and it can sometimes be quite helpful.
After a ferry disaster at sea, some relatives of victims whose bodies
had not been recovered asked to be taken on a boat trip around
the sunken ship. They wanted and needed to see the place where
their loved ones had been killed.

> It's not a terrible dream or figment of my imagination.
> This is where it all happened and this is what it did to
> me. I can now see that it is real.

Such a trip is usually very distressing, but it can help the
process of grieving to continue and enable people to identify more
closely with the loss and trauma that they feel. The whole process
of identifying with the incident, in whatever way, is important. It
must be seen as real so that those involved can know that their
reactions are the result of a specifically distressing event.

Sometimes survivors and relatives feel detached from their
feelings and from the reality of what has happened; visiting the
scene helps them to see that these feelings are not made up or
artificial. They do have a focus in the event and in the loss. This
can come through contact with the dead or through visiting the
scene of the accident or disaster. These are important rituals that
help people experience their pain.

Talking about the experience

Encouraging people to talk is one of the main ways of helping
people admit to and express their feelings. However, it is common
for others not to mention the event in a mistaken attempt to avoid
causing embarrassment or hurt, although the embarrassment is
often theirs and not that of the victim.

Many people who have been involved in an accident or disaster, or who have been bereaved, have a burning desire to talk about their

Most do talk if they are given the opportunity.

experiences or about the person who has died. Occasionally, because of the shock and numbness, some will not talk about it and they retreat into themselves. But most do talk if they are given the opportunity.

Experiencing the Pain

Again, the intention is to counteract the problem of denial and the tendency to hide feelings and emotions. The following helps those who have been involved in a trauma begin to accept the reality of what has happened:

- Be specific and direct about the incident.

- View the body if appropriate.

- Visit the scene.

- Encourage those involved to talk.

Although some who have been through a traumatic experience might try to avoid the reality of what happened to them, these steps help present the facts plainly, so they can see the reality for themselves. This should help them express the pain in the symptoms of post-trauma stress and grief.

People should not be told to control their emotions, nor should they try to avoid what they are feeling, however uncomfortable. "Don't cry" and "Don't be upset" are not helpful and can even cause more problems. It is important to treat the survivor, victim, casualty or the bereaved in a way that tells them clearly that what they are feeling and experiencing is normal.

A grieving or otherwise traumatized person must not be made to feel that he or she is ill or sick. The person may need constant reassurance that he or she is not stupid, weak or going crazy. This reassurance can come through very strongly from others through their attitudes and in the way they are reacting and behaving. Helpers should try to convey empathy, and also that the reactions are normal. Certain things will make victims aware of the situation and may help them to express their feelings and emotions.

The importance of rituals

In the case of a death, viewing the body and the funeral are important events, which often release emotion and feelings. They are usually in safe surroundings usually, with the priest, minister or rabbi present and the family gathered. This gives mourners permission to grieve and express emotions. The whole process of arranging the funeral, the service in church and the burial or cremation, usually helps the pain to emerge.

Visiting the site of the incident or disaster can be a ritual with effects similar to those of visiting a grave or attending a funeral. Memorial services and ceremonies have been held after some accidents and disasters. These useful rituals help people to express their grief and loss.

Saying the wrong things

Helpers should encourage people to express their pain by making affirming responses to what is said. Negative responses only make matters worse by denying the reality of the feelings and sending the message that it is wrong to express emotion.

> Some weeks after Jean's baby had died, she attended a formal dinner. When she arrived, a friend, trying to be helpful, said, "My goodness, you look absolutely terrific this evening." Jean said afterward, "I could have hit him. What he didn't know was that I felt awful and empty inside, I didn't feel terrific."

Comments such as this and "Don't worry; time heals," or "I know just how you feel—the same thing happened to me" are attempts to help. But they can hurt because they can stop grief from coming out into the open; feelings get buried away even deeper inside. On the positive side, statements that diminish one's feelings can have the effect of making people even more angry and upset. If they can express this anger and upset, then they may also get in touch with their painful feelings. However, the helper will probably be the focus of the anger and become even more defensive. "Don't yell at me. It wasn't my fault. I only came here to help." Saying the wrong things can have a number of results.

- The victim, perhaps feeling vulnerable and looking for advice, accepts what the helper says, and keeps her feelings under control by repressing them. She believes it is wrong to express emotions. "The minister and the doctor told me, so it must be true."

- The victim becomes even more angry and upset and directs this at the helper. This can cause the helper to retreat.

- The victim becomes very angry, but only after the helper has left and so she feels even more frustrated, guilty and isolated.

- The victim silently rejects the helper and puts up mental barriers against any help whenever the helper calls.

When the initial feelings of shock, unreality and denial combine, sometimes they prevent underlying pain from being felt or expressed. Talking might not get through this barrier, so anyone trying to help should be patient and sensitive to the reactions and feelings being expressed. However, it is important for the helper or carer to be present with the survivor, because their presence alone can give comfort and help if they refrain from saying the wrong things.

> A woman whose 9-year-old girl had been killed in a traffic accident commented that people often said the wrong things to her. Her advice was, "If you can't think of anything to say, don't say anything, but just touch their arm. Someone did that to me and it meant more than a thousand words."

It is also important to get the facts right if you do say anything. Victims, survivors and the bereaved are usually in a very sensitive state. If you get names, places, events and other information wrong, they can take it as a sign that you don't really care, or haven't bothered to find out, or weren't listening.

It is especially important to get names or relationships right, because these are of prime importance. If my husband or baby is dead, then getting this information wrong is an insult to their memory.

That said, it is fortunate that some sufferers are extremely forgiving and compassionate. Some may be so numbed and shocked that whatever you say doesn't register anyway.

Saying the right things

- Say you are sorry about whatever has happened, and, if possible, get the facts right.

- Don't feel you have to talk. Just be there and touch an arm or hold a hand—if they will allow you to do this—but not in an intimate manner unless you know the person very well.

- If you don't know what to say, say nothing.

- Don't be afraid to mention the accident or disaster or talk about the one who has died.

- Don't prevent the person from talking about what he has experienced or is feeling. Be prepared either for no response at all or a flood of words and emotions. If the person does wish to talk, encourage him to do so and get him to talk about the incident or the person who is injured or dead.

- Ask if you can do anything to help—make a cup of coffee or place any telephone calls—but don't make the person feel that he is incapable of doing things for himself.

Adjusting to the Changes

When someone close to us dies, we lose part of ourselves. It's natural to have to adjust so that we can survive without this person. Such a loss can be like losing half of your body or personality: "I don't know who I am. Part of me has been torn away. He isn't there with me any more." In marriages, families and close relationships, as well as with friends and colleagues, we are who we are because we actively relate with them and to them. They help us to laugh and to cry, to be happy or sad.

We are at the center of a huge circle of relationships in which others play a part and interact with us and with each other. They determine to some extent who and what we are, depending on the nature of our relationship with them. It is like living on the end of a huge seesaw, with our loved ones, our life beliefs and the people and things we have become attached to balanced at the other end.

If one of those people or things suddenly falls off, we crash to the ground. How strong that crash is depends on the strength of the relationship. The seesaw is unbalanced, so we have to move along and adjust our position again to restore the equilibrium. In a similar way we cope with trauma when, we hope, our lives otherwise are reasonably balanced; we have beliefs about ourselves and the world and a purpose in life to help us cope.

When the basis of our lives is challenged or threatened by changes, accidents or disasters, we can become unbalanced and unable to cope. The balance needs to be restored. Two theories about why some people may manage to cope better than others are based on the ideas of *projection* and *identification*.

Projection

Where individuals have developed a high sense of self-esteem throughout their lives, they tend to be able to cope on their own, and they seem to have a better chance of surviving and adjusting to trauma and loss. When someone feels that their identity is separate, this is usually because they have an inner strength and confidence that enables them to cope better than others. This seems to be true of people in marriages and relationships and may be relevant for those involved in accidents, disasters and other traumatic situations.

In bereavement and grief, the response of people in this category is usually to say, "Something has been torn from inside me." These people have lost part of themselves, but because they have this inner personal sense of their own identity and worth, they find it easier to adjust and cope. What they have lost is gone, but they themselves are still very much "here."

Identification

Some people can be described as "clinging" in their relationships with others. They usually have a very low sense of self-esteem, and they find it difficult to cope on their own. They have attached themselves very firmly to someone or something else and taken this inside them. They have identified this other person with themselves. They cannot exist without them. They cannot bear to be separate because their sense of worth is invested in another. This "other" might be a person, a belief, a way of life or even a job, a house or some other object. Their view of themselves is to say, "I cannot live without you because without you I am nothing."

When they suffer loss, these people tend to say, "Something died within me." Their feeling is not that something has been taken away from them, for what has died or been lost remains dead inside them. What they have lost has not gone away. This feeling can result in a reduction in the ability to adjust to trauma and loss of any kind.

It appears that those who have a high sense of their own value and worth tend to cope better with loss than those who do not.

However, if those who suffer are given the opportunity, they should be able to feel the pain of the trauma or loss and grow to accept what has happened. Some think that they will not be able to carry on with their lives, but most eventually find that they can cope, no matter how hard it is to do so at first. As time passes, they learn that they can survive. Knowing that you can survive can bring a feeling of relief, but it may also be tinged with guilt at having been able to cope.

Once they have begun to adjust their emotions and feelings they might discover that they can do things they have never done before. Somebody who was content to stay at home can suddenly travel the world. A person who was always happy to stay at home may join groups and clubs. He or she might even find a new lease on life and become a fitness fanatic, go ballroom dancing, horse riding, cycling, skiing or find some other hobby or interest. However, for some this change does not happen. These

Knowing that you can survive can bring a feeling of relief, but it may also be tinged with guilt at having been able to cope.

people experience intense loneliness and isolation for a very long time and may even hide from others, including relatives and friends. Yet many of them, if they are given support, do learn to cope on their own.

Sandra's husband was killed in an accident. When the funeral was over, friends visited her regularly and within a few days had told her that she should be getting out and about. They belonged to a community theater and tried to get her to join. "It'll be good for you," they said, "you'll meet new people and maybe find a new interest." When she declined their invitation, they called a number of times and tried to get her to change her mind.

Then they suggested that she go on a vacation, and when that failed, they said they would take her to an exercise group every Thursday. This didn't work, so they told her she must find something to do outside. "You have to get out and not mope in the house. It'll only make things worse for you. You should be starting to enjoy yourself." Eventually they gave up asking and making suggestions and told people, "We've tried to help her, but she won't help herself."

In fact, Sandra was grieving, and because she was doing so, she was coping quite well with her loss. She did cry and felt lonely and depressed, but her daughter and son visited regularly to support her. They didn't interfere, however, and allowed her to take things slowly. They enabled her to retain her independence and self-respect. She could cope because she had a caring and loving family around her who allowed her to mourn and wept with her. They talked about their father and often laughed at his sense of fun and spoke of the many things they had done together: the vacations and the hard times, the happy times and the many changes they had shared

as a family. It took time, but almost two years later,
Sandra found herself a part-time job in a local store and
had made friends with a widower who lived a few houses
away. She was surviving and coping very well.

Helping people adjust to their trauma or loss does *not* mean
urging them to get out and do things or trying to force them to be
happy. If they are beginning to accept what has happened and
have learned it is all right to feel the pain, even if it is sometimes
almost overwhelming, they should then be moving along the road
toward finding out for themselves how they can adjust. Some will
want to make drastic and major changes in their lives; usually these
changes should not be done too soon. In general it is unwise to
move soon after an incident unless it is absolutely necessary, or to
form intense new relationships or move into a marriage within a
few months. This is because people's emotions and feelings might
not be too stable and they can make decisions that they will regret
when they have begun to recover.

Generally people need time to be able to move through their
feelings and most, with some help, will find their own way. The
way to help them is to ensure that they are beginning to accept
what has happened and beginning to feel the pain. If they do both
of these things, they will probably find their own ways of
readjusting. If we attempt to impose our own solutions on them,
we might be taking away their ability to cope and only increasing
any feelings of inadequacy.

Redirecting Emotions

When we begin to recover, to feel that life has started to take on a
new meaning and that we can survive, we face the problem of
what to do about our emotions, feelings and needs. It is like being
left with a huge bag full of things that we need to give away, but
we don't know who to give them to or how to give them away.
They seem locked inside us.

However, by the time we have moved to this stage it is likely
that we have already begun to share our lives with significant
people and have found some new interests. We felt isolated and

alone at the beginning, even though many others were around to help, but gradually we have been able to talk and share our feelings. Redirecting our emotions is a gradual process. Our emotions emerge slowly over a long period, and eventually we find that the balance in our lives is beginning to be restored.

Patricia's husband, Bill, was killed in a work accident when he was 50. She was 46. Their two daughters were married and had their own families in the same area. During her marriage, Pat had relied almost totally on Bill, and he had done everything except the cooking and ironing. She was a "homebody" who rarely went anywhere without her husband. At first, she was devastated. She collapsed completely and her family had to do everything for her. Even nine months later she would sit in her chair and say very little, although she was able to read novels. She said that she still felt that Bill was going to walk into the house at any time.

Liz, a friend who had been at school with her and lived in the same town, heard about Bill's death, so she began to visit regularly. They shared memories of their childhood days and how as young girls they had both met their future husbands at the same factory. Liz was also a widow and they started walking together. This progressed to visits to the local restaurant for a drink and to the movies. Pat was wary of men, and felt that if she started another relationship the same thing might happen again. She wondered if another man would be like Bill.

She knew inside that, although she had loved Bill, he had taken over her life and dominated her. She had always resented it, and this had made her feel that she could not cope. She was able to talk to Liz about this, and slowly she gained confidence in herself. With Liz, she joined a class at the local college, where she studied English literature. After 18 months, she met a man in the group who took her out frequently, and their relationship became very close. They both wanted to be sure. Pat had been supported by her family, who were there giving practical help and allowing her space and time to grieve.

Meeting and being with Liz helped her to go out and mix with others at a safe distance. Talking with Liz and sharing memories enabled Pat to look back over her life and marriage. The interest in literature grew from her love of reading and led to meeting Jim, whom she married two years later.

At times we might suggest to someone that they might like to do this or that, but we must do it sensitively and carefully, bearing in mind their vulnerability and need to be in control of their own lives. We must not try to run their lives.

Sudden deaths

Sudden deaths are common in accidents and disasters and can cause special problems for survivors and relatives. They cause a strong sense of unreality and an even stronger feeling of guilt. There can be an increase in the need to blame somebody, in the feeling of helplessness and a deeper depression than might be expected. Survivors and relatives can ask many questions.

- "If only I had seen her once more before she died."

- "Did she know that she was dying?"

- "Did she say anything before she died?"

- "I feel terrible. We had a fight this morning, before I left for work, and we both said some awful things to each other. If only I could make things right with her."

- "I wish I had been a better husband to her. If only I could start over."

- "Why can't I see him just once more so that I can tell him how sorry I am, and how much I love him?"

- "Why do the hospital and the police have to be involved?"

- "What's it got to do with them? I don't want my baby/husband/wife/mother touched or messed with."

Sudden deaths seem to increase and intensify the usual feelings of grief and those who help will need to use different approaches.

Helping after sudden death

There may be the need to be almost aggressive in offering help. You will certainly need to be assertive.

- Offer help without asking whether it is wanted or needed. Treat the situation as if it's normal that those affected by the trauma should be helped. Many clergy and other helpers visit without asking whether their visit is wanted. Most say that they are never turned away. This can help counteract the natural resistance and defenses of the bereaved.

- Be specific about the accident or disaster and talk about it, even if they try to avoid it. Ensure that the loss is made clear, and use the word "dead" or "died" as with other grief.

- Because sudden death increases agitation and the sense of vulnerability, people need to talk even more than ever and should be encouraged to do so. Making people physically comfortable is also important.

- Always make the offer of follow-up support and visit regularly, whether you are made welcome or not. Continue to visit, not just for weeks but for months and even years. Some clergy, doctors and other carers keep a register of the dates of accidents, disasters and deaths, and visit on the anniversary or send a card. A visit is better, although some will say that this only serves to remind them of the event and bring back the pain. In terms of coping with pain, this can be helpful, because it might unblock feelings and help to lower defenses. However, in this event make sure additional support available as needed; people should not be left high and dry.

Conclusion

The most difficult thing for anyone to understand about the reactions to trauma and loss is that the responses, of whatever kind, and the pain contain within them seeds of renewal and healing. If we are allowed and encouraged to experience this intense pain and suffering, and the many complex feelings and emotions that emerge, we can slowly come through the trauma and feel that life is worth living again. We know that life for us will never be the same, but we can adjust to new ways of living and coping.

Those involved in traumatic incidents, whether as rescuers and helpers or as survivors, and their relatives or the relatives of those who are killed, should be aware of the effects of the trauma on them and on others, so that they can eventually learn to cope and get on with their lives. The methods discussed above are effective when used with anyone suffering trauma and loss, not just from accidents and disasters, but also from other losses in life. A particular method for helping through psychological debriefing will be discussed in the final chapter of this book.

Further Reading

Deits, Bob. *Life after Loss: A Personal Guide to Dealing with Death, Divorce, Job Change & Relocation*. Revised Edition. Fisher Books, 2000.

Lewis, C.S. *A Grief Observed*. San Francisco, CA: HarperSanFrancisco, 1995.

Peck, M. Scott. *People of the Lie: The Hope for Healing Human Evil*. New York: Simon & Schuster, 1997.

Pennebaker, James W. *Opening Up: The Healing Power of Expressing Emotions*. New York: Guilford Press, 1997.

Selye, Hans. *The Stress of Life*. New York: McGraw-Hill, Inc., 1978.

Who Is Involved?

A BASIC PROBLEM IN UNDERSTANDING AND COPING with post-trauma stress is the denial and resistance encountered in

- Society in general

- Survivors and victims

- Helpers and carers

- Those in authority

Among these are two basic core groups.

The believers

Believers think that, like other responses to trauma and loss, post-trauma stress is a natural and normal reaction and is not necessarily a sign of weakness or personal inadequacy. They see the need for education, understanding and awareness for everyone, especially for helpers, rescuers and carers, and for help through special counseling and psychological debriefing (or critical incident stress debriefing—CISD).

This group believes that it helps to

- Prepare for incidents with awareness, training and cooperation among organizations and agencies

- Provide support at the time to help defuse the situation

- Use psychological debriefing as a standard procedure and normal response two to three days later, with any follow-up as necessary

- Include as many people as possible, including survivors, rescuers and helpers, in the debriefing

The resisters

This other group consists of those who tend to feel that post-trauma stress is the invention of psychologists and others, and that it is symptomatic of modern life and attitudes. Resisters believe that post-trauma stress is the result of a drop in standards in society and is a sign of a decrease in any sense of responsibility or real strength of character. Some also take the view that because of recent changes in society, many people are less able to cope than people of previous generations. For them, the answer to post-trauma stress lies in the rediscovery of old moral values and standards and in encouraging people to cope through not giving in to crisis and carrying on despite difficulties.

> The "I coped and so should you" attitude is neither helpful nor realistic.

There is also the tendency to deny that there are such things as depression, anxiety or stress, except for those who show signs of weakness or who lack moral purpose or strength. Sufferers are those who are weak-willed and have been brought up in a society that has gone "soft."

The response of some in this group is to say things such as, "We went through the last war and we didn't have any of this nonsense. People just went ahead and made the best of it." However, the reality is that it is impossible to say how many people's lives, health, relationships and marriages were damaged or destroyed because of their war experiences. There is no doubt that some returned and found it almost impossible to adjust to the changes that had taken place during their absence—changes both in themselves and in their families. Some could not get back into their marriages or former lives and found it even more difficult to move forward. Wives and families had learned to cope on their own and found support from others, with a husband and father absent in some cases for a number of years. Perhaps one of the differences between the two world wars and those of recent times is that the whole nation was involved and there was a feeling of mutual suffering and support, whereas the Vietnam and Gulf Wars did not involve everyone in the same way.

Many thousands have developed psychological, emotional and physical problems of one kind or another from all the previous wars of the twentieth century up to Vietnam, the Gulf War and the Somalia conflict of recent years. There are also the strains and stresses of living in a society where shooting, robberies, accidents, terrorism, murder, intimidation and bombings seem to be a constant threat.

In addition, there has been a lack of understanding of the nature of trauma and loss and of the specific reactions and problems they cause. We have seen great advances in our understanding of the process of grief and of responses to trauma. These insights show that the "I coped and so should you" attitude is neither helpful nor realistic. It has already been argued that the macho image is very strong in our society and is presented as a defense against either showing or admitting to having feelings. This is especially true within uniformed, male-dominated organizations. The main problem lies in the prevalent attitude that you must not show any emotions—you should just get on with life without whining or making a fuss.

However, because of our increased understanding of the reactions to trauma and loss and the knowledge that expressing feelings is a necessary element in the process of recovery, such a belief and attitude is counterproductive and inevitably makes it more difficult to cope.

All people face the typical traumas and stresses of life just by being alive. These kinds of traumas are as normal as a family fight or argument, or as ordinary as driving a car. In these situations, stress is a useful reaction, because without it we would not survive the fights or the trip. The right level of stress enables me to stand up for myself in a

> *Stress becomes a problem when it causes distress and an inability to cope.*

confrontation or drive safely in a world where everyone else on the road behaves like a lunatic! Stress becomes a problem when it causes distress and an inability to cope.

This may come through involvement in situations that are outside my capabilities or experiences, such as new and difficult changes in life, or as the result of an accident or disaster. These situations are possibilities for all people.

If we add to these a stressful job, then any problems, either at work or at home, may be magnified. In time of crisis we can be more at risk of experiencing stronger traumatic reactions than at other periods in our lives. Those at special risk are those whose work entails the additional stresses encountered by involvement in traumatic events.

It's important to note that many of these professionals do cope most of the time and are able to carry out their duties efficiently, without falling apart or having the experiences destroy their lives. Do not suppose that these professionals all walk around with deep and unresolved problems that blight their lives and ruin their health and relationships. Their training and professionalism, sense of duty, pride in their work and the knowledge that they belong to a specialist group enables them to cope. However, it can be argued that the very things that help them to cope may also result in an even stronger than normal defense mechanism of denial and the repression of their thoughts and feelings in some instances. Also, all will experience stress at some level and some will suffer from post-trauma stress. Some will suffer in silence and others will need and ask for help, but resources to help them might not be available. The first task when working with people in this situation is to understand the pressures of their work and the special nature of their duties and then to ask what strategies they use in order to cope.

The Police

By the very nature of their work in responding to the needs of the public in times of crisis, police face many stressful areas of life. These include

- Violent family situations
- Child abuse
- Murder and suicides

- Informing next of kin of deaths
- Violence against individuals or groups
- Armed robberies, muggings and fights
- Hostage situations
- Shootings and sieges
- Rape and violence against women
- Attending accidents and disasters
- Attending post-mortems and inquests
- Riots and strikes
- Terrorist activity
- Violence and physical abuse against themselves

Like others, police also experience the normal losses and traumas in their private lives. A policeman who is having marital or family problems or is going through a divorce or separation may find it more difficult than usual to cope with his work. Colleagues may be aware, because of his behavior, that all is not well. It's also natural to ask how police officers, like any other professionals whose jobs involve maintaining public safety, can work during a particularly traumatic incident—where they see the mangled bodies of men, women and children and the reactions of survivors—and then go home and relax with their families.

Most do cope, but in what ways and how does it affect them? After the Lockerbie air disaster, the local police and the army, among other services, were called in to help. Most soldiers came from the same regiment, knew each other well, had trained with each other, had their own chaplains with them and had a strong sense of solidarity. Many of the police were not local, but were brought in from other areas and then returned home each day. The soldiers worked together, slept together, ate together and stayed together, and so could to talk and share their experiences and feelings late into the night. The police traveled home, either on busses or in their own cars, and there was almost no opportunity for many of them to talk and share what they saw and felt.

Because of these differences, some believe that the soldiers were better able to cope with the traumas they faced each day. Newspaper accounts reported that police officers involved at Lockerbie suffering from post-trauma stress had increased rates of absenteeism, poor health and problems in relationships. It would be interesting to know the reactions, experiences and opinions of their spouses and families. It seems that a cohesive and closely knit group of people are more likely to cope in a traumatic incident than individuals who do not know each other, have not worked together before and do not have much opportunity to talk to each other.

However, it could be argued that because of these same differences, the soldiers were better able to hide and control their true feelings and only talked about things on the surface. It could be that the cohesiveness of a group enables its members to cope better *at the time*, but that some may develop problems later which only emerge occasionally in symptoms with an unacknowledged cause or source. Did they show their real feelings and express them, and therefore not exhibit many or any of the symptoms of post-trauma stress, or were they simply better at repressing their real feelings?

Training and cooperation are also important factors. There is little doubt that the emergency services, including the police, who help in disaster-recovery efforts can cope better when they train together on a simulated disaster exercise prior to an accident.

The police have their own support services and some forces already have, or are looking very seriously at having, professionally trained counselors skilled in psychological debriefing to help police personnel not only after accidents, disasters and major emergencies, but also following other traumatic incidents. There is also the support, typical in all uniformed organizations, provided by the chain of command—those in positions of authority normally feel a sense of responsibility for their people and will look after and be interested in their welfare.

Police Officers and Post-Trauma Stress

A special web site devoted to police officers coping with post-traumatic stress is found at this address:

http://pw1.netcom.com/~jpmock/ptsd.htm

However, it is not sufficient for senior officers to ask their men and women into their office to check that they are okay and to let them talk for a little while after a difficult incident. This step does show that the senior officers care, but the "checkup" needs to be done in a more professional and structured manner, as is provided through proper psychological debriefing.

Police personnel may not want to tell their superiors how they feel or discuss their problems with them. This is probably because of a macho-style self-image, anxieties about the opinions of their colleagues and the effect of a "confession" on their personal reports and therefore, their careers. In any case, the typical post-trauma-stress reactions and natural defense mechanisms of denial will be operating after a traumatic incident, even if those involved appear to have few concerns about their images or future. Properly trained support is essential.

Fire and Rescue Services

Like the police, the fire and rescue services are involved in accidents and disasters, and they may have to extract victims and survivors from buildings or vehicles. They may even be called upon to rescue a child or a cat from a tree or a child with his head trapped in a fence or railing. On some occasions they will face situations of extreme danger and risk their lives on the job. Although they are highly trained for such emergencies, it still means that they experience life-threatening incidents and therefore stress and trauma. They put their own lives in danger, see survivors and the dead sometimes in a badly burned or mutilated condition, and they will be expected to cope with all that.

A conference on coping with trauma was attended by members of the emergency services from a number of counties. Some fire and rescue officers said that, in their unit, they believed they were able to cope and did not need special counseling or help. They felt that because they worked on "watch" in teams, they were able to share their thoughts, feelings and experiences when they returned to the station. This, they said, meant that they did not have any great problems and were helped to cope.

However, what they were talking about was "defusing" and not "debriefing." We can ask the same question as before: Did they talk at a deep level and really say how they felt, or was the talking a way of defending their true feelings and emotions, even if it helped them to cope in the short term? Methods for coping at the time and shortly after are not the same as dealing with the feelings and emotions generated. Some coping methods may result in burying the feelings deeper inside.

> *Did they talk at a deep level and really say how they felt, or was the talking a way of defending their true feelings and emotions, even if it helped them to cope in the short term?*

Also, if women are present as part of the team, will this cause the men to be more defensive than normal, because they feel that they have to cope in front of women? Or will the reactions of the women, who may be better able to show their feelings, help them to feel that they can safely talk more openly? It's also possible that the women, instead of being able to bring out their feelings and express their emotions in this situation, will try to be like the men and show that they also can be "strong."

Men

"Women are present, so I must be strong and not show any signs of weakness . . ." "The women are being emotional, so I must be strong for them and be a shoulder to cry on." "The women are crying and upset, so that gives me permission to do the same."

Women

"I'm a woman so the men here won't mind if I cry." "I'm a woman, but I will show these men that I'm not weak. I won't cry or get upset."

Debriefing is for everyone

Fire and rescue services do have some internal support systems in place. Some areas do have personnel trained in counseling and psychological debriefing and some debrief as standard procedure. Psychological debriefing must be for everyone and not just for those who may seem to be suffering. Part of the problem is that if they are given an opportunity to choose, many will probably

> *Psychological debriefing must be for everyone and not just for those who may seem to be suffering.*

decline the invitation and these may be the very ones who most need help. Having debriefing for all as normal, standard procedure removes the need to ask and can counteract the defenses of denial.

Ambulance Crews

Ambulance crews also work at traumatic situations: accidents, disasters, shootings and bombings, heart attacks, attempted or successful suicides or murders, medical crises, deaths, pregnancies, births, miscarriages, abortions and a variety of incidents where there is violence, abuse or injury. They are normally involved in incidents where the police and fire and rescue services are present. Like those in the other professional services, these men and women are highly trained and usually work in pairs in one vehicle or in teams with men and women working together.

Their lives may be at risk occasionally, and they see suffering and death at close quarters. They work erratic hours, often on standby, and this condition increases the likelihood that they will experience stress and trauma. Sometimes their work is extremely frustrating, especially in those cases in which they may have to remain at some distance from an incident to assess needs or in which they are unable to save a life.

These frustrations put ambulance workers under further strain. Their needs are exactly the same as those of the police and fire and rescue services. They require training in awareness of the effects of post-trauma stress, support and aftercare following involvement in difficult situations. After some incidents, they will need counseling and psychological debriefing.

Emergency Services Workers and Post-Trauma Stress

A Critical Incident Stress web site dedicated to emergency-services personnel, including firefighters, nurses, ambulance teams and police, is found at this address:

> http: // www.geocities.com/CapitolHill/Lobby/3082

The Armed Forces

Members of the armed forces, like other professional services, are trained to carry out a job they hope they will never have to do. In their case, this means preparing to fight the enemies of their country. In addition, they give aid to the civilian community in times of crisis, such as disasters and accidents, floods, air crashes and national strikes. Sometimes, when soldiers are involved in peacekeeping activities, they become targets for gunmen and rioters.

They also help in hostage situations, shootings and in defusing bombs. The most stressful situation for them is usually in time of war and when involved in peacekeeping activities such as Somalia or the Balkans. Terrorist activity also means that wherever they are stationed, their spouses and families are seen as "legitimate targets."

Further stress is caused by long periods of separation. It is not unusual for some to be away from their families more than nine months out of each year. They can move around frequently, especially in the army, disrupting their home lives and affecting schooling, friends, neighbors and work opportunities. When they are stationed abroad, spouses have little or no access to their own families back home in times of need.

Members of the armed services have the support of chaplains, doctors, social workers and the entire military support system, but the traumatic effects of all the pressures in the lives of service personnel, no matter how minor, are felt by their spouses and children also. Although many soldiers feel that they are doing a useful job when they are in a peacekeeping assignment, they also face the fear of death or injury every day, separation from their families and sometimes extreme verbal and physical abuse and violence from the very people they are supposed to protect.

They perform their duties in the belief that they are protecting society from the activities of terrorists, and they approach their work with dedication and a strong element of good humor. They may recognize that they are using humor as a defense mechanism for coping with the more difficult feelings the situation arouses in them.

The Vietnam and Gulf Wars resulted in an additional area of stress. Many members of the soldiers' extended families suffered anxiety and looked for support and help because a son, daughter, brother, sister or other relative was serving their country so far away. In some cases, members of the armed services, and other organizations, have to face the death of a friend of colleague, and this can result in a group as well as a personal loss.

The death of someone in a unit can cause grief to many others, including those in the chain of command. Those in positions of authority may feel guilty and responsible. This can cause even stronger reactions of denial. Senior officers and the senior ranks sometimes react by believing that, because they bear some the responsibility for the death, they should remain strong for the sake of their men and not show any signs of weakness.

> A young but fairly senior officer who had commanded men in a war situation attended a church service at which the chaplain spoke of a lack of responsibility and care among some commanders in certain situations during World War I. Whatever the point of the sermon, this officer, who could only barely remember World War II as a boy, objected strongly to the criticism and took it personally.
>
> He said that some of his men had been killed and that it wasn't his fault. He was in quite agitated. He was having difficulty in coming to terms with the fact that when he had been in command, some of his men had lost their lives. He was torn between what he saw as his

responsibilities as a commander who should remain
strong and unmoved, and his personal sense of grief, loss
and possible failure.

Commanders in all organizations quite naturally can become
very defensive about their responsibilities and decisions, especially
when people are hurt or killed. The response can be to say that it
wasn't their fault, that they were only doing their duty, and that
someone had to make the decisions. This may cause strong
reactions of denial of feelings with the result that they decide that
they, or their men, do not need help. In some cases the response
is to say that there have not been any reactions of stress or loss.

If any stress or loss reactions are admitted, then it be that the
comments come from those who "cannot cope" and who "should
not be doing the job in the first place." This further strengthens the
"strong and silent" image, but can result in repressed emotions and
more problems at later. The organization of the armed services
provides an excellent basis on which to build a counseling and
debriefing system, because extensive support already exists.

However, because this system and the image it encourages is
entrenched, it is easy to agree with the powers that be and to
believe that psychological debriefing is not necessary. This
perception is strong, not only at among the lower ranks, but
throughout the services, where it can reinforce or produce the idea
that only "wimps" need help. Also, if the tendency is to believe
that only those who have personality defects or are inadequate
need help, there can be a strong idea that any support should be
provided through the psychiatric services and so a medical and
psychiatric model is used.

Under this concept, people show signs of stress or trauma
should be sent to a doctor and a psychiatrist should be consulted.
When an incident occurs, the system can mean that those in
command look at the responses of the people involved and then
decide who does and who does not need help. The danger in a
hierarchical, rigid organization such as the army can be that those
in command feel responsible and so must make the decision, not
only about who needs help, *but also about who should give it.*

Seven of my men were involved in a bombing in which one of them was killed. The rest were all injured. Four seem to be coping well, but two are extremely upset and, of these, one is almost overcome with grief. Therefore, these two must see a psychiatrist, but the others are all right and just need to see a doctor.

The problem with this thinking is that it is not possible for anyone to make this kind of judgment just by looking. The men who are coping might be the ones who are reacting strongly, whereas those who appear calm may not be able to keep their feelings locked inside forever; at a later stage their feelings may affect their work, health or families. It is much more effective to have psychological debriefing as standard operating procedure for everyone.

No one will be labeled as needing psychiatric care, for all responses will be seen as normal. When everyone is included, no one has to suffer the humiliation of having to ask for help. Should anyone need further help, they can seek assistance from a doctor, psychiatrist or therapist. I believe that the helping model should not be medical or psychiatric, but multidisciplinary and carried out by specially trained personnel.

Each area, district or command could have a team of selected and trained debriefers, centrally supported and funded, who can be called upon whenever there is a critical incident. The armed services could do this easily with little cost and enormous benefit to the personnel concerned.

> *I believe that the helping model should not be medical or psychiatric, but multidisciplinary and carried out by specially trained personnel.*

Not only will the men and women of the armed forces benefit from an across-the-board approach, but also it will help educate the public about the benefits of debriefing. The specter of the homeless Vietnam vet suffering from post-traumatic stress many years after the war ended can serve as a constant reminder to the importance of this activity.

Fortunately, the armed forces has shown a growing awareness of the emotional reactions sparked by traumatic situations and a great deal has been and is being done to help those who suffer from post-trauma stress. Each of the services has a group of psychiatrists and clinical psychologists who specialize in traumatic stress and in helping those who suffer. In Great Britain, during and following the Gulf War, a multidisciplinary team was created and trained to carry out psychological debriefing with those who had been held hostage and with the soldiers who handled and buried the dead. Perhaps this debriefing will become standard procedure in the future, not just for those involved in war or peacekeeping actions, but for any who suffer traumatic events.

Prison Workers

Prison officers live in a very special environment where men and women are forcibly separated from their families and the rest of society for long periods. The officers are also part of this system and usually work in an enclosed and disciplined community where feelings of isolation, loneliness and threat are common.

These men and women move constantly between this environment and their own home. Like those in the other services, these workers can feel that they live in two separate worlds—the world of work, where there is sometimes threat and violence, and the world of their homes with their families, where there should be freedom and normal family life. They also are trained to cope with their special work circumstances, but still they live under stressful conditions.

Stressful conditions might be expressed in relatively minor cases of frustration and anger or by a full-scale prison riot, such as one at Strangeways in Manchester. This riot was partly the result of the conditions in the prison, such as overcrowding and the humiliations of emptying slop jars, seen by prisoners as dehumanizing. Some staff members also believed this. Prison officers may have to live in a world where they are not happy about the conditions, but they have to make the best of it and accomplish their duties efficiently and effectively. The riots at Strangeways showed that in some cases there was an extremely strong sense of identification on the part of the staff, not just with their colleagues and the prisoners, but with the prison itself.

Strangeways represented their whole lives and livelihood, and they had dedicated themselves to their work to the extent that the riots and subsequent destruction of part of the prison buildings meant a deep personal loss for them. It was as though a part of them had been ripped out or, like the prison, torn down. Trust and cooperation had been built up and then broken. Some staff members had strong reactions typical of post-trauma stress.

Newspaper stories have told of officers at this prison suffering emotional, health and marriage problems in the aftermath of the riots. Prison officers are trained to deal with riots, but they also have to cope with a fairly high level of stress in other areas of their work. They can face intimidation and threat, often veiled and not obvious, and anxieties about their own and the prisoners' living and working conditions. There can also be stress caused by the difference between their work and home environments. Sometimes they have to cope with suicide, murder or violence among inmates, and they may have problems accepting and overseeing certain types of prisoners. When they face traumatic incidents, they need support and help during and following the event. This can be provided by their own chaplain and social services, but also through psychological debriefing.

The Media

Newspaper and television reporters also face stress in their work, for wherever the above-mentioned services are found, members of the press are there too, looking for news stories. Obviously, such news involves pain and loss for other human beings. Media people are also human beings, and the incidents they deal with can cause trauma and stress for them. Photographers and reporters in situations of war, disasters, accidents, deaths, murders, droughts, famine, floods, tornadoes, robberies, acts of terrorism and other sensational and dramatic events must be affected in some way, no matter how immune they might think they have become.

They can retreat behind the screen of professionalism and of "getting the job done," but there is no doubt that some reporters are deeply influenced by their experiences. We only have to think of some who went to Ethiopia and Africa and returned so deeply affected by what they saw that they were instrumental in raising money for famine relief.

Some who took part in the Vietnam and Gulf Wars have said that their lives will never be the same again. Sometimes the media is criticized for sending photographers and reporters to the scene during and after traumatic incidents. It has even been alleged that some reporters and photographers have dressed as clergy or doctors to gain access to victims and information.

It may be that the demands of their work sometimes push them to do things they wouldn't normally do. Allegations about reporters tricking or lying to others to get at a story may or may not be true, but it needs to be asked whether the involvement of the media is helpful or harmful to victims, survivors and rescue workers.

Obviously, there can be occasions where onlookers, bystanders and other would-be helpers may prevent rescuers from doing their work. Similarly, the activities of photographers and reporters are sometimes intrusive and disruptive.

However, survivors and relatives can be helped by the knowledge that others are interested in and care about their problems and troubles, especially when the story, with photographs, reaches the daily or local papers, the radio or the television news. Publicity can also result in very positive responses from governments and organizations when injustices have been done, and many have been helped because a newspaper has publicized their case and cause.

It can be that after an accident or disaster, or an event such as a murder, suicide or death, the press can help survivors and relatives to receive compensation or the satisfaction of knowing that something might be, or is being, done.

A sensitive press can help sufferers to know that others care, but a sensationalist press can do much damage and can deepen the trauma for survivors and their families.

The problem can be that survivors of accidents and disasters, and their parents and relatives, are often in a very delicate and fragile state. They may be suffering from shock and symptoms of hysteria or numbness. Their reactions and feelings can be dulled so that they agree to be interviewed or give information shortly after the event, or they may actively seek and demand attention and publicity, all of which they might regret later.

Occasionally, their response is of extreme anger at what they see as an intrusion into their personal, private grief and suffering. A sensitive press can help sufferers to know that others care, but a sensationalist press can do much damage and can deepen the trauma for survivors and their families through their intrusion and sometimes aggressive behavior in the pursuit of newsworthy items. In the field of post-trauma stress, the press, radio and television have been instrumental in raising public interest and concern, especially after the Vietnam and Gulf Wars and because of their coverage of the hostages in the Middle East and elsewhere.

Much publicity was given to the return of the hostages in the Middle East and of their need for help, understanding and debriefing. This heightened interest in all of the public sectors and services and prompted a general realization that people can and do suffer from post-trauma stress and need help. A major step in my life was appearing on a television program some years ago related to the effects of stillbirths on mothers and fathers. Many similar programs on subjects such as bereavement and loss, child abuse and rape and the effects of accidents and disasters on ordinary human beings, have changed the attitudes of people at all levels. The media therefore have a great responsibility not only to bring news to the public mind and eye, but also to produce their reports fairly, due to the fact that what they do can influence the attitudes and opinions of so many people.

These are only a few of the organizations and services whose members face stress and trauma regularly in their work. Much could be said about air, sea and mountain rescue teams, coal-miners, oil-rig workers, merchant seamen, doctors and nurses, clergy, Red Cross volunteers, social workers, teachers, counselors and many others whose work sometimes means encountering tragedy and loss.

These professionals can be exposed to the same stresses and traumas as those in the services mentioned above, and they can have the same or similar reactions both in themselves and from their superiors. All need to be aware of the affects of critical and traumatic incidents on themselves and on others and of methods of coping.

Husbands, Wives and Partners

When we ask who is involved in a trauma, we need to keep clearly in mind that we must include spouses and partners. It is easy to forget them and think only of the immediate victims and rescuers. Many of these people have wives, husbands or partners that they will return to once the incident is over. Those who are not married or who do not have partners still have families, friends and colleagues. The stories of some of those mentioned in this book show clearly that partners and children of victims and helpers are involved and influenced by the trauma.

> Louise was sitting watching TV late one evening when the news suddenly reported live from the scene of a terrorist incident. To her horror, she saw her husband being carried on a stretcher to an ambulance. The immediate effect on her was one of shock and disbelief.
>
> She went through the procedure of being officially informed that he had been injured and that one of his colleagues had been killed. She had to visit him in the hospital and go through the long, slow process of recovery once he returned home to convalesce. He had to cope with the trauma of the incident and the injuries he suffered, plus the death of his friend.
>
> He also felt guilty about having survived when his friend had been killed and the fact that he was now out of work and an invalid at home. His wife had to try to come to terms with her own shock and depression and her feelings of anger and resentment. Both had to cope with their own feelings as well as those of their partner.

This story shows that the victim or survivor and the rescuer and helper are at the center of the incident, but they are surrounded by those nearest to them in their families. All of them will be influenced in some ways by the event.

Wives and families of helpers can believe that the husband or father should be able to cope because "that's his job and he should be used to it." Wives and husbands of victims and helpers can become bored, angry, annoyed, apathetic and irritated by the behavior of their partner.

The effects on relationships have been listed earlier in chapter 4 and in Appendix C, but the following are of special note.

- An inability or unwillingness to discuss things, resulting in terrible fights and arguments or a retreat into isolation.

- The relationship can become very uncertain because life seems unpredictable, like the partner.

- There can be constant anxiety and worry about money, security and the future.

- Either one or both can discover an increased or decreased desire for physical affection.

- Partners can blame themselves and believe that it is their fault, or they may blame the other person. This can cause guilt and shame and feelings of being useless, rejected and unable to help.

- The anger and frustration can build up and explode and be directed at the other person, at children or at someone or something else.

- Panic is not uncommon, especially when people feel so helpless, and there may even be bouts of excessive spending or meanness.

- Partners can change and develop a new self-image or seek a new way of life.

The problem is that like the reactions to grief and loss, traumatic responses can have both a negative and positive effect. Some will deepen their relationships and need for each other and draw nearer in their care and concern, while others will drift apart and search for more satisfying or less demanding relationships.

Children

How do children react to trauma in themselves and in response to trauma in other family members? Sometimes it is difficult or impossible for them to say how they feel, so they find other ways of showing or expressing their feelings.

Play

Children seem to find it easier to act out their feelings through what they do and in how they behave rather than in what they say. Some will become uncharacteristically aggressive in the way they play their normal games and in their relationships with their friends. In addition, they might even invent or find new games to play, especially games involving violence, such as playing soldiers or war games, being involved in an accident or playing the role of someone in authority such as a policeman, soldier or doctor.

Children seem to find it easier to act out their feelings through what they do and in how they behave rather than in what they say.

One 4-year-old boy, who had been involved in a hostage situation in which his father was still being held, was playing with plastic building pieces. He had made a little figure of a man with a large number of small white blocks attached to his head. When he was asked why, he said that this was a man who had been hurt and that the white blocks were bandages on his head.

He was too small to explain his fears, so he probably acted them out in this way. Other children retreat into their own world, becoming quiet and uncommunicative, lose their appetite, play by themselves or in their own rooms and shun contact with friends. They might also be aggressive with parents or destroy toys or other playthings and be demanding and disruptive. Another way of expressing how they feel is through drawings or paintings.

Some psychologists specialize in art therapy with children who have been involved in trauma or who are suffering because of another member of their family.

> A little girl whose father was away for a peacekeeping
> mission had drawn her own picture of "Daddy as a soldier,"
> and she put this picture on her bedside table in front of his
> photograph. She told her mother that the picture would
> only be taken away "when Daddy comes home."

She was acting out her anxiety and worry in this small but
dramatic way. Other children will draw or paint violent situations,
such as accidents or people fighting, or produce paintings with
themes suggesting anxiety and worry or anger and sadness. Some
psychologists specialize in art therapy with children who have
been involved in trauma or who are suffering because of another
member of their family.

Expressing feelings

Feelings may be expressed through play, drawings and unusual
behavior. However, as well as expressing worry and anxiety,
children can blame themselves. This can happen after accidents
and disasters, but also because of other changes in life, such as a
divorce or separation, or the death of a sibling, friend or other
family member.

Children can project problems between their parents outside,
onto others, or internalize them through a process called
introjection, in which they may blame themselves and believe that
the problem is their fault. Introjection can result in withdrawal or
anger and in the need to be punished by being naughty or
disruptive in the home or school.

Children may show their anxiety
through an extra sensitivity to
criticism from parents, friends or
teachers. It is helpful for parents to
know that this behavior is not
abnormal, but a reaction to inner turmoil. Children may need more
hugs and cuddles than usual. They need reassurance that they are
still loved, and still lovable.

Children may show their anxiety through an extra sensitivity to criticism from parents, friends or

Some will accept this love and caring, but others might reject
physical contact or comfort and this can be very difficult for
parents to cope with or accept.

Children might also complain of minor illnesses, such as stomachaches, headaches and feeling tired, or an inability to relax or sleep, or not want to go out or go to school. Even older children might return to an old teddy bear or toy from the past or to some pattern of previous childhood behavior such as thumb-sucking, clinging to a parent, crying or, in some cases, bed-wetting. They may also have bad dreams or nightmares.

> *Teachers report children show unusual behavior not only when the child has been in traumatic situations, but also when the parents have been.*

Teachers report children show unusual behavior not only when the child has been in traumatic situations, but also when the *parents* have been. Even the child's perception that the parent may be in danger can affect their behavior. It can also happen to children of people who are under stress from their work, such as policemen, fire and rescue personnel, ambulance staff, prison officers and members of the helping professions and organizations.

Any changes in behavior can be significant, but should not always be seen as abnormal. They are responses to stress. These and other reactions can be found not only in children involved in accidents, disasters, divorce or when a family member is suffering or has died, but also when some major change is about to or has taken place. These include losing a pet or friend, moving, school changes or going into or coming out of the hospital.

Many people share the misconception that children do not suffer grief or loss. This idea is untrue; children are as much at risk from the trauma of grief or loss as anyone else, except that they may not be able to say or express how they feel. Those involved closely with children as parents, family members or teachers need to be extremely sensitive to the child's needs and reactions and, if possible, provide reassurance, security, comfort and understanding.

> *Any changes in behavior can be significant, but should not always be seen as abnormal. They are responses to stress.*

The Problem for Helpers

Helpers have two main problems; first, they must do something, and second, if they can't do anything, they can feel a sense of failure. Those who are not trained in counseling are especially prone to feel that they have to be seen to be doing something. If they can't, they may feel useless.

This can also be a problem for those who are, or believe that they are, in positions of authority and leadership. They may feel that they should have the answers or solutions to problems because of who and what they are and also because others expect this from them. Traditionally, clergy and doctors have been looked up to by others as people who have access to special authority and to solutions, whether from God or from some source of all healing and knowledge.

It can be difficult for them and those in similar positions to face situations where they feel, or are, helpless. There is nothing they can do except to stand back and wait, or to pray, and even this can be thought of as a pointless and futile exercise—because it isn't seen to be doing "something." One method of coping, typical of stress reactions, is to practice denial.

Professionals can easily retreat behind their roles and erect barriers that keep people and their problems at a distance. The clergy can hide behind a clerical collar and retreat into ritual and ceremony and the authority of their office. Doctors can use their professional status, the white coat and stethoscope, the hospital organization or the receptionists as a shield. When talking about counseling and debriefing, a priest said

> I don't need any of this counseling or debriefing nonsense. Whenever I come across any pastoral situation where there is a problem, be it a death, marital or personal problem, I take with me two thousand years of Christian spirituality.

Another responded by saying

> I don't use any of this counseling or debriefing stuff. My job is to preach the gospel wherever I am. That's what I do.

Both responses avoid the issue and threat of real involvement and helping by retreating behind the barriers of the Church, the priesthood and the gospel. In the stage play *Whose Life Is It Anyway?*, the doctor, chaplain and hospital social worker are all criticized because they treat the patient (an artist paralyzed from the neck down) as an object and not as a human being. They all hide behind their professional cloaks. The doctor believes that he can make decisions for the patient and force him to have injections. The chaplain tells the patient that he should be grateful that he's a cripple because others will feel good when they help him. When the artist becomes angry and abusive, the female social worker talks about how the room is decorated. All avoid the reality of the situation and avoid real involvement.

When they are involved following accidents and disasters or bereavement, loss or any traumatic events, both clergy and doctors need to remind themselves that they also are human beings. They can help best, not by retreating into their own perceived professionalism, but by being there and showing they care. They can use their own professional skills and knowledge, understanding how trauma and loss affect individuals, families and themselves. They can develop the skills of listening and responding to those in need. By being aware of the method of helping through psychological debriefing, clergy and doctors can either carry out the debriefing sessions themselves (if they have the time and skills) or refer people to others who can.

After accidents, disasters and other traumatic incidents, survivors, and in some cases their families with them, should be debriefed, either in the hospital, at home or elsewhere. This should be part of the standard procedure and response to a disaster.

Earlier I mentioned a young man who was in a hospital following a car accident in which his best friend was killed. The doctor and chaplain in the hospital told him that it wasn't his fault and therefore he must not blame himself. He should put it behind him and get on with his life without any feelings of guilt, shame or anger. Had these professionals been able to use the skills of psychological debriefing themselves, or had available someone who knew the skills of psychological debriefing, they would have been more helpful to their patient, and the young man would almost certainly not have been suffering to the same extent weeks later.

How Do Rescuers and Helpers Cope?

Rescuers and helpers of all kinds have strategies for coping with the experience of being involved in traumatic incidents. These strategies are largely defensive and enable them to work effectively and, where possible, save lives. This must be their first task. However, they are not always aware of these strategies, but information and research shows how some helpers have coped at the time of the incident and later.

Although the paper discussed here concerns working with traumatized children, it should be of interest to all who help in other incidents, and the strategies used are similar. Following a bus crash in Norway in August 1988, in which 12 children and three adults were killed, Dyregrov and Mitchell produced a report entitled *Work with Traumatized Children–Psychological Effects and Strategies for Coping*. The reactions are typical of carers and rescuers in other situations although the point is made very strongly that dealing with dead or traumatized children is especially stressful.

> Seeing the bodies of dead children leads to significant emotional distress even in the most experienced helpers. But even in more routine work in hospitals, dealing with traumatized children intensifies stress in the worker.

A questionnaire was sent to all who worked at the site of the accident, asking them about their responses and how they coped. It also asked for information about their role at the time, their previous experiences of accidents, if any, and their reactions during the first few weeks following the incident. This report is significant and important for those who work in situations of trauma and stress and can throw some light and understanding on personal and group methods of coping.

Coping Strategies

Being active

Ninety-four percent believed that by doing something and keeping themselves busy they were able to curtail their feelings and prevent themselves from thinking about what they were doing. It was significant, but logical, that during rest periods or when they were trying to relax, this strategy didn't work, because thoughts and feelings began to come to the surface.

Mutual support

Ninety percent mentioned the importance of the support they received from their friends and others at the site. This was particularly through close physical contact. Touching each other and talking were important for them and raised their morale.

Suppressing emotions

Seventy-six percent said that they were able to make conscious efforts to suppress their emotions and shut out their feelings.

Unreality

Sixty-eight percent reported that the shock created very strong feelings of unreality. Most were unaware at the time that this feeling enabled them to cope. If it was unreal, then they could continue. One person said that he felt "like an actor in a movie."

Avoidance

Sixty-eight percent said they purposely avoided thinking about what they were doing and emotionally detached themselves from what they saw. Some even thought of the children as dolls in a training session.

Preparation

Sixty-three percent tried to prepare themselves for the event once they had been told they would be helping, but some imagined that they would be dealing for the most part with old people.

The fact that they might have to deal with children was not in their minds and came as a shock. However, they felt that mental preparation had helped them to cope.

Knowing what to do

Forty-eight percent said that their training helped them cope because they felt competent and capable and knew what to do. This reassured them and raised their morale.

Regulating exposure

Thirty-eight percent coped by limiting the amount of time they spent being actively involved. Some did not seek information, but preferred to remain ignorant of some details. "What I don't know can't hurt me." Some focused on one specific task at a time and avoided what was going on around them. Some also thought of something else, such as working in the yard at home.

Having a purpose

Twenty-four percent thought that if they didn't do the work, then someone else, perhaps less skilled, would have to do it. This justified their involvement. There was also a sense of purpose and the knowledge that they were doing it to help children.

Humor

Sixteen percent said that they had used humor to cope. This represents a much lower percentage than humor usually rates in other events.

These strategies are normal reactions, and they suggest that helpers and rescuers do have or develop internal methods for coping, some of them conscious and others unconscious. Training, preparation, acquired skills and previous experience are very important, plus a sense of solidarity, closeness with other helpers and mutual support.

This means that uniformed organizations, with their own special training and the knowledge that they belong to an efficient and competent group, are likely to cope better than those without any of these qualities. Everyone involved in critical incidents, including those responsible for training and support, should be aware of these strategies and strengths so that they can build on and develop them and be better able to cope under the traumas and stresses of their work.

Common Reactions among Helpers

Dyregrov and Mitchell report that although there were some reactions at the time, most helpers said that their main reactions only developed once they had left the site.

Helplessness

Sixty-seven percent said that they felt almost completely helpless. This was difficult because their expectation as rescuers and helpers was that they should and would be in control. Working with children reminded them starkly that they could do little or nothing to change what had happened. They felt that they should have been able to do more.

Fear and anxiety

Seventy-five percent of those who had children of their own or children they loved felt especially vulnerable. They were frightened that the same thing might happen to their loved ones and they tended to become anxious and overprotective of their own children. In the psychological debriefing that followed the event, some said that they had to keep looking into their children's rooms to make sure that they were all right. In some cases, this worry caused sleep disturbances.

Sense of unfairness and injustice

The deaths of children are seen as "a direct insult to a helper's assumptions of an orderly and just world. Since children are unable to protect themselves, their suffering is seen as unjust and unfair." We expect our children to bury us, and not the other way around. A paper in 1988 by McCammon and others ("Emergency Workers' Cognitive Appraisal and Coping with Traumatic Events," *Journal of Trauma and Stress*, 1988) shows that an important coping strategy among rescue workers and helpers is the search for meaning. Because the death of a child is out of sequence in life's expectations, it is difficult for it to make any sense.

Rage and anger

Helpers and rescuers can direct anger and rage at those who seem to be responsible for the accident. Exposure to traumatized children can have other effects on helpers and carers who may become "more critical, intolerant and less trustful of others" (Dyregrov and Mitchell). Ordinary problems of life can seem trivial and cause irritation, and the anger might be directed at families. This is rather similar to the response mentioned earlier, in which a man was involved in a riot and his wife asked him if he wanted steak and potatoes or a hamburger and fries that night for dinner. His response was one of anger because the question was irrelevant and trivial when compared with the trauma of his experiences.

Sorrow and grief

Some helpers may become immune to the deaths of adults, but this is not true of those involved with children, where there can be responses of extreme sorrow akin to that of a personal bereavement. Crying was common, and some said that when they went home and saw their own children, they burst into tears. It is also significant that helpers will more readily accept crying and distress as a reaction to working with traumatized and dead children than with adults.

> *It is significant that helpers will more readily accept crying and distress as a reaction to working with traumatized and dead children than with adults.*

Intrusive images

When helpers, carers and rescuers are asked what incidents they remember from their experiences, they usually talk about having been involved with children. From this report it is evident that images and pictures were impressed on their minds. "We carried two dead children in our ambulance. From one of the stretchers a leg with a yellow sock was visible. Now I see yellow socks everywhere."

Self-reproach, shame and guilt

Many asked questions about how they performed their duties. Had they done enough and could they have done more or done it in a different and more effective way?

Positive Results

More than 33 percent said that as a result of the accident, their sense of value had increased and that life had become more precious to them. One year after the event, almost 45 percent said that their lives had changed in meaning, and they had come to appreciate their loved ones more, especially their children. They also said that they had been surprised at the strengths they had found in themselves and in others. Other reports produced after disasters and accidents produced similar findings.

They also have a great desire to be helpful to others. These qualities mean that they have to help and therefore use conscious and unconscious strategies for coping. The main method of coping in an accident or disaster is to use "emotional distancing" and when this does not work, for example in extremely distressing cases, it leads to the breakdown of natural defenses. Coming across a dead child can cause these defenses to collapse. Also, carers and helpers tend to identify with victims, and especially with children. Instead of saying, "It could have been me," they say, "It could have been my child."

Childhood events can influence present responses, and some helpers when working with children unconsciously remember their own childhood separation anxieties and fears. The problem can be that helpers may see themselves more as substitute parents rather than rescuers or carers and this can have deeper emotional consequences.

The conclusion by Dyregrov and Mitchell is that rescuers, helpers and carers perform effectively, "as long as they continue to be active, have concrete tasks to perform and are able to keep the emotional ramifications of the event at a distance." This strategy of "distancing" enables them to cope during the incident, but does not prevent reactions at a later time.

The paper also discusses the use of humor by helpers, and the conclusion is that when dead or traumatized children are involved, humor is seldom used as a defense. After a certain transportation disaster in the North Sea, researchers Alexander and Wells found that 98 percent of police officers working in the mortuary used humor as a defense in order to cope. In another paper, Hetherington and Guppy found that 93 percent of police traffic officers also used humor as a coping mechanism.

The strategy of "distancing" enables them to cope during the incident, but does not prevent reactions at a later time.

This was not true in a Norwegian bus accident that was studied, because it involved children and also because onlookers and survivors were present. However, humor is a normal and helpful way of coping because it can "reduce tension, keep emotional distance and build group cohesion and morale when performing arduous tasks" (Dyregrov and Mitchell). Thus, humor seems to be a common coping method except in situations where children are involved. In the Norwegian accident, only 2 percent said that they used humor "very much," 16 percent said that humor was used in moderation, 24 percent that it was used "somewhat" and 60 percent "not at all."

When children are present in accidents or disasters, defenses and reactions are stronger than usual, but the use of humor as a coping strategy is greatly reduced. Dyregrov and Mitchell also say that talking about experiences and feelings with colleagues after the event was particularly helpful.

Humor seems to be a common coping method except in situations where children are involved.

> Clinical experience gained from providing follow-up debriefings for disaster workers in this and other accident and disaster situations highlights the need for confronting the event following the disaster work. While distancing is most helpful at the scene, the reverse seems to be most helpful afterward. By actively confronting one's impressions and reactions through meetings and conversations with colleagues and others, the helper is

able to manage the aftereffects of trauma work in the
best possible manner. (Dyregrov and Mitchell)

This "best possible manner" is through psychological, or
critical incident, debriefing, which provides a structured method of
talking through the experiences and feelings of those involved.
This debriefing should *not* be done on the day of the event or
immediately after the work is over.

> During these times, many helpers still function in the
> emotionally distanced mode . . . they need to change
> from reacting with their brain to reacting with both brain
> and heart. (Dyregrov and Mitchell)

This method of helping people to cope applies equally to
survivors and, in some cases, will help families and others involved.
Therefore, the people involved in a traumatic incident can be
someone falling off a horse, a person whose marriage has just
broken up and their partner and children, a soldier returning from
duty in Kosovo, a policeman who finds a mangled body in an
accident, a fireman who rescues someone from a burning house, a
counselor with a client who was involved in a bombing, the friend
and family of a young man who has
committed suicide, or the victims and
helpers in a major disaster. It can
include all these people and those who
come into contact with them—families
and friends, neighbors and colleagues.
Any or all of these are potential victims and may experience some
of the symptoms of post-trauma stress. They will need support,
counseling, and debriefing.

*While distancing is
most helpful at the
scene, the reverse seems
to be most helpful*

Further Reading

ASVP Staff. *Critical Incident Stress Debriefing-PAL*. Mosby-Year Book. Inc., 1991.

Fossum, Merle A., and Marilyn J. Mason. *Facing Shame: Families in Recovery*. New
York: W.W. Norton & Company, Inc., 1989.

Raphael, Beverly. *When Disaster Strikes: How communities & individuals cope with
catastrophe*. New York: Basic Books, 1986.

Psychological Debriefing

AFTER A SITUATION THAT CAUSES TRAUMA and stress, a number of people will be involved, from a child falling off her bicycle and running to her mother, to large groups of people after a major disaster. This can include the victims and survivors, police, fire and rescue, ambulance services, doctors and hospital staff, witnesses and bystanders, volunteers, counselors, clergy, social workers, various community support services, Red Cross and ambulance personnel, psychiatrists, psychologists and many others in an ever-widening circle. At a later stage, help and assistance might be provided by other organizations. In a minor incident, only a few of these might be involved.

> Jane crashed her car into a tree, but she was not injured. She was interviewed by the police and advised to see a doctor, but apart from two pedestrians who stopped to see if they could help, she did not speak to anyone else at the time. When she went home, she was able to talk about this event to her husband and friends, and they were sympathetic and helpful. Within a short time, Jane was back to normal and driving again. However, she drove extra carefully for some time afterward.

In a major disaster, large numbers of people are involved, including relatives, friends and the general public. I remember clearly where I was and what I was doing when President John F. Kennedy was assassinated in 1963, and I can also remember that on March 6, 1987, I was at a party with some Australians when we heard about the terrible ferry accident at Zeebrugge.

Because of instant media coverage, especially television, people in their homes can be brought to the scene of a disaster almost immediately. We have seen on television vivid and disturbing pictures—sometimes live as well as on tape—of a horrifying variety of gruesome shootings, bombings, fires, earthquakes, floods, tortures, airplane crashes, tornadoes and kidnappings.

The pathetic sight of survivors and the devastation, destruction and carnage caused to people and places, a child's toy, a handbag or an article of clothing, or the bodies of victims, can bring strong emotional reactions from those who have no direct involvement other than watching television in the comfort of their own homes. Any major incident can have effects that are like the ripples on a pond when a stone is thrown into the water. They spread out in a widening circle of influence, affecting all they touch, until the energy is gradually dispersed.

Methods of Helping

People can be helped to cope with traumatic events in a number of ways.

Self-help and awareness

Self-help for victims, rescuers, helpers and others is created with knowledge, preparation and training. Rescuers and helpers need to be trained to cope not only with the incident, but also with their own and others' reactions at the time and later. Victims, survivors and their relatives can be helped by already knowing about post-traumatic stress reactions and by being aware that such responses are normal.

General education on grief, loss, stress and trauma for everyone, including school children, is essential. It can be done through the media, school and training in the workplace. The methods discussed in chapter 6 of coping with trauma and loss, which are similar to those used in grief and loss reactions, will also be helpful for all.

Defusing

This is the procedure during the incident where there is mutual support and caring, and an opportunity after the event to gather informally to talk through what has happened.

Psychological or critical incident debriefing

This is the main subject of this chapter and can be used with individuals, couples, families or groups. It is a process that should take place no sooner than 24 hours after the incident.

There are methods used particularly with those who are suffering from post-traumatic stress disorder and these are discussed at length in chapter 6 of *Coping with Catastrophe,* by Peter Hodgkinson and Michael Stewart. They include

- Behavioral treatments, such as desensitization and exposure to the fear, flooding techniques and training in methods of relaxation

- Cognitive therapy, in which the aim is to correct unreasonable, distorted and unhelpful beliefs

- Psychotherapy, which attempts to deal with the anxiety caused, the defense mechanisms generated and the feelings that are buried and hidden

- Group therapy, which sometimes includes residential care and treatment

- Medication, which normally should be used in conjunction with the other methods mentioned above. It has been especially successful when combined with psychotherapy.

Initial Problems

For those not suffering from post-traumatic-stress disorder, the most positive help is to encourage them to talk about their experiences and feelings to a good listener or counselor and to have support and understanding from families, friends and colleagues at work. However, a more structured method of assisting called *psychological debriefing* or *critical incident stress debriefing* (CISD) is also an option. This raises a number of problems, not least is the implications of the titles.

Denial

One of the natural reactions to loss and stress already discussed is that many will deny that they, or others, have any problems. Therefore, words such as "psychological" and "stress" suggest the need for treatment and can strengthen the denial.

> I don't need help. I'm just fine, thank you.

> My people are professionals. They are well trained
> and don't suffer from stress.

Those who are involved in a traumatic incident and the people responsible for them may be using the defense of denial when they say they are coping and do not need help. It should be stressed that many will cope through their own inner resources and with the help and support of their families and friends, but it needs to be acknowledged that the effects might continue for some time and be buried deep inside.

The title

The words "psychological" and "stress" have various stigmas attached to them, even for those who don't deny that there is such a thing as stress or trauma. To some people, "psychological" suggests craziness, nervous breakdown, being crazy, mental illness, instability, going out of your mind, insanity, weakness or character deficiency.

> I don't want anything to do with shrinks.
> There's nothing wrong with me.
> I certainly wouldn't want that on my record.
> I never suffer from stress.
> I can cope just fine, thank you.
> I don't want to be labeled a head-case and I don't want
> to see any shrink or do-good counselor.

Following a certain hostage situation, a number of people involved were offered debriefing. However, the authorities called it "counseling" and, understandably, the response of many was to say firmly, "No thank you, I don't want to be counseled. I don't need treatment." The word *debriefing* is also a problem for some. In the armed services and other uniformed organizations, it usually means a meeting following an incident or exercise, concerned with either giving or obtaining information, or sharing ideas, experiences and opinions.

There is not usually any reference to feelings or emotions. An interview carried out by the police after an accident or other traumatic event with a survivor or victim is largely concerned with finding out what happened and what those involved can remember. The problem can be that if someone is traumatized, it can either be difficult for him or her to remember, or the story pours out like a flood. It might be difficult to avoid the feelings.

Often if you ask someone what they *thought,* they tell you what they *felt.* That's entirely different because they immediately switch into their emotions. In most cases the police are acutely aware of this, although it can be very difficult for the interviewer to remain detached enough to obtain the information without being overcome by the emotional content. The suggestion is also made that the word "counseling" should be used—critical incident counseling—but counseling and psychological debriefing are not the same.

> *Counseling and psychological debriefing are not the same.*

Counseling is sometimes a long-term process, whereas psychological debriefing, based on the Dyregrov and Mitchell model, is meant to be a one-time event carried out in a highly structured and disciplined manner with the possibility of a follow-up. This is discussed later. Because of the problems I have described, some believe that people will be more accepting of the process if it is referred to as *critical incident debriefing,* because it avoids using the words "psychological" and "stress," but here I will use the term *psychological debriefing.*

The method and model

Whichever method or model is chosen for helping those who are involved in traumatic incidents, there are difficulties to face. Some people will refuse to talk about their experiences and feelings and will keep them locked up inside—while others will talk for hours. Psychological debriefing is usually done in a group setting where everyone is given an opportunity to speak, but a few will find this threatening and will not wish to meet or talk with others.

They will avoid even those who shared the experience of the disaster with them. Some of those who feel this way may talk eventually, but they feel safer if they open up with someone who is "neutral:" not known to them, not involved and not someone from their own organization or unit. Some people who are suffering stress or trauma will probably not want any of their peer group or those in authority to know in case it affects their image and future.

> *Psychological debriefing is usually done in a group setting where everyone is given an opportunity to*

To have debriefing as the usual and normal procedure for everyone can put some of these fears to rest. The Dyregrov and Mitchell model and method of psychological debriefing can be adapted for use after any traumatic situation, from a relatively minor accident to a major disaster. It is not concerned with the scale of the incident, but instead with how people have reacted to the incident and what the incident has done to them. The model can also be used with an individual, with couples or with a larger group.

Who Suffers?

Keep it firmly in mind that most people will cope by using some of the various defense mechanisms discussed in chapters 5 and 6, but that all will feel the effects in some way. Denying this truth implies the belief that only those who are seen to be suffering will need help. *Yet you cannot just look at people to determine who is or who is not suffering.* Physical injuries are usually visible or detectable, but psychological stress and trauma can be well hidden. Those who are shouting and screaming and crying and talking might be the ones who are coping best because they are able to express their feelings and emotions and bring them out into the open. Someone who is quiet and calm may be suffering inner turmoil and confusion and be keeping a firm grip on reactions of shock and horror.

Psychological debriefing, if it is accepted as normal procedure, can surmount the problems suggested by these differences because it is something that is intended for *everybody involved*, not just for those who appear to be suffering. A debriefing group will usually consist of some who are coping well, others who are having difficulties and a few who might have long-term problems. The message that needs to be repeated continuously until it is understood and accepted is:

> *Physical injuries are usually visible or detectable, but psychological stress and trauma can be well hidden.*

PSYCHOLOGICAL DEBRIEFING IS FOR EVERYONE

Organizations and institutions should include psychological debriefing as the normal procedure for all who share in the traumatic experience. In an accident or disaster, the survivors and those working at the site of the incident are the most obvious people at risk. So, debriefing should be for survivors, rescue workers and helpers first, as a priority, but those on the periphery of the incident may also benefit from debriefing. At the very least, they should know the possible effects of what's happened to their relatives or friends and how this can influence them too. Others will feel the effects in some way and they are even farther out in the circle. Starting at the center, moving gradually outward, a comprehensive list includes

- Survivors
- Helpers—police, fire and rescue, ambulance services, and so on
- Bystanders and witnesses
- Carers—including doctors, nurses and clergy
- Families and friends
- Work colleagues and neighbors
- Debriefers and other helpers—trained debriefers, counselors, social workers and those from other social-services and caring agencies

All will need some help and support, if not debriefing.

Defusing

It is essential that helpers are trained and prepared to the greatest extent possible for critical and traumatic incidents. Their sense of belonging to a professionally trained group will help them cope, as will the support they receive from each other before, during and after the event. They will use their own particular defenses for coping at the time, but will be helped afterward if they also can talk to those who worked with them. Also, it helps if they can gather for routine meetings to talk through their experiences during the incident and once it is over.

Defusing can be done informally.

This process is called *defusing*. It creates an opportunity not only for them to talk to each other, but also for them to think about discussing their emotional reactions. At this stage they do not normally need professional counseling, and the defusing can be done informally by some member of the team, possibly one of the leaders. The services of organizations such as the Salvation Army in providing cups of coffee and cookies or sandwiches during the incident also give an opportunity to talk and share experiences and are a valuable element in helping people to cope.

Clergy and medical staff can also be present and, as well as giving spiritual comfort or medical help, they can be useful in giving verbal and physical support, understanding and encouragement. Immediately after the incident, those involved are often not in any condition to be able to deal with their experiences, so there should be no attempts to criticize and no excessive use of humor or boisterous behavior.

It's important *not* to carry out the psychological debriefing immediately, because people will not be able to cope with it that soon. Dyregrov and Mitchell have said that at this stage, victims, rescuers and helpers are thinking with their heads rather than with their heads and hearts. Preferably, the debriefing should take place after about 48 hours.

Psychological debriefing can be done later than this, but not so late that the feelings and emotions have become internalized and mixed up with other things.

Psychological Debriefing

Psychological debriefing can be defined as

> A meeting with one or more persons, the purpose of
> which is to review the impressions and reactions that
> survivors, helpers and others experience during or after a
> traumatic incident such as an accident or disaster.
> (Dyregrov)

The aim is to give an opportunity for people to talk and share
their experiences and feelings, to reduce any aftereffects and also
to minimize the possible development
of post-traumatic-stress-disorder
symptoms. The model of debriefing I
suggest is that produced by Dyregrov
following other work by Mitchell. The

Preferably, the debriefing should take place after about 48 hours.

value of this model lies in its flexibility, in that it can be adapted to
suit many different situations, from a relatively simple incident
involving one or two people to a major disaster. The important
elements in debriefing are as follows.

Debriefing Is for Everyone

Debriefing should be seen as the normal caring response to all
who have been involved in a traumatic incident—survivors,
witnesses, helpers and carers and, sometimes, their families. It
should be standard procedure. The armed services, police, fire and
rescue and ambulance services in particular should have debriefing
written into their operating instructions and orders. A number of
hostages who returned from overseas said

> When we stepped off the plane we expected three things.
> First, a medical checkup to see if we were physically okay.
> Second, a normal debriefing about our experiences. Third,
> we wanted to talk about what we have been through and
> how we were feeling. We had the first two, but not the
> third.

For example, after a traffic accident, a debriefing could be
carried out with the police officers involved, the ambulance
personnel, and perhaps other helpers. This would probably be

hard to do because it would require crossing the boundaries of different organizations. At the least, however, each group could have its own system of using debriefers.

After a bank robbery, all those working in the bank could meet together for a general debriefing. In the case of the chaplains' meeting for a debriefing after a riot, all the clergy attended, even those who were not there at the time, because they belonged to the team and had been drawn in emotionally throughout the incident and afterward. They all felt that they were involved and were touched by what had happened.

The here and now

The debriefing focuses mainly on present reactions and feelings. This will result in discussing and looking at the incident, how it happened, what people saw and experienced and how they feel about it now.

Mobilizing Resources

The multidisciplinary approach

The approach to debriefing should be multidisciplinary. It should not be labeled as the domain of any particular specialists. Post-trauma stress is not exclusively a medical, psychological, spiritual or social condition, but can contain elements of all of these. It is important not to medicalize, psychologize, spiritualize or socialize the debriefing, because people can then assume that they are ill and feel that they need special help from a doctor, psychiatrist, priest or social worker. Psychological debriefing should be done by those who are trained in the procedures, whatever their other professional orientations or skills.

> *Post-trauma stress is not exclusively a medical, psychological, spiritual or social condition, but can contain elements of all of these.*

One solution would be to have a nationally organized and multidisciplinary team of trained debriefers who could be called upon when needed. They could be selected from many organizations and disciplines and then trained in the debriefing model. Those in authority often resist this idea because they see the procedure as threatening their leadership capabilities or discipline.

The benefits of debriefing

It can be pointed out, especially to those in positions of responsibility or who hold the purse strings, that debriefing has certain specific benefits. It can reduce

- Short- or long-term distressing aftereffects, particularly the development of post-traumatic stress disorder

- The incidence of sickness and absenteeism

- Personal, marital and relationship problems

- Problems at work

- Anxieties about how people might cope and what help they will receive after an event

- Anxieties for any who might feel threatened or embarrassed by asking for help

- Anxieties about stress and traumatic reactions being seen by others as signs of weakness

Perhaps as important as any of these is the knowledge that the organization does care and is using techniques that will help. The positive trade-off in terms of time and money can be enormous, and any company or organization should see the benefits of this process.

Education

All staff members, at all levels of the organization should enroll in educational programs that are designed to make them aware of the possible reactions to stress and trauma. It's nice to make leaflets and booklets available. Banks have training sessions that prepare the staff for robberies and hold-ups, but these corporations should also include information on how these incidents are likely to affect their workers.

Trained debriefers

Professionally trained personnel to carry out the debriefings is essential. These can be people from inside the organization, selected and trained, provided they meet the following requirements. Debriefers should

- Be carefully selected and trained

- Belong to a support group

- Be working under supervision with a tutor-consultant

- Be trained counselors

- Have knowledge of group structures and dynamics and experience in working with groups as well as with individuals or couples

- Have knowledge of post-trauma stress and the possible effects on individuals, groups and families

- Thoroughly understand the debriefing model and know how to adapt it to their situation

Some counselors may feel that they do not need all this background and that their skills and experience should be sufficient for them to cope with the demands of debriefing. However, debriefing is *not* the same as counseling. Counseling techniques and methods are used, but have to be applied within the formalized structure of the debriefing model. Normally, counseling involves a series of sessions, usually for a limited amount of time such as an hour, which takes place over a number of weeks or months, or longer.

Psychological debriefing involves one or more sessions set within a formal structure carried out, at the earliest, within two to three days of the incident taking place. It can last for a morning or afternoon, for a day or longer. The debriefing of a team of chaplains after a serious prison riot was carried out in the relaxed surroundings of an old country house over two days. The debriefing of a family held hostage took three hours. Debriefers may be consultants working on a part-time basis, whose advice is sought and who are called in when needed.

The Psychological Debriefing Model

- Debriefing can be carried out by one debriefer, but two debriefers can be used to greater advantage, possibly one male and one female.

- Because the session is open-ended and might continue for some time, it is a good idea to make sure that all participants have made a visit to the restroom beforehand.

- Coffee-making facilities should be available.

- A rule should be agreed upon and established about smoking.

- Participants should sit around a table, all in similar chairs, including the debriefer. Being around a table rather than in an open circle removes the possible impression that they are attending a therapy session. An open circle is also much more threatening to some.

- No observers, press or others should be included.

- Participants should be told that if they wish to leave at any time they are to do so quietly, but leaving early should be discouraged.

- They should be told that it will be a long session, lasting hours, without a break.

- When the group is gathered together in a place that is suitably relaxing, comfortable and private, the leader takes charge.

Introduction

After a short self-introduction the leader, and co-debriefer, if present, talk about personal experiences of debriefing. This helps create confidence at the beginning of the session.

The rules

The following rules are made clear.

- *You do not have to say anything* besides what your role was at the time of the incident, and why you were there.

- *Confidentiality is emphasized.* There should be no note taking, unless by mutual agreement. If notes are taken, a record of the meeting can be sent to members of the group afterward. Nobody outside will be contacted without the permission of those in the group. Those taking part must agree not to talk to anyone outside about what happens in the group.

- *The main focus is on reactions now.* It is stressed that although past experiences and feelings will probably emerge, the main emphasis is on impressions and thoughts as they are expressed and felt in the group.

- *Feeling worse.* Those taking part should also be warned that they might feel worse during and after the session, but that this is normal.

- *Complaints.* It should be explained that the group is not a forum for dealing with complaints and moans—of which there will probably be many.

Procedure

Those taking part are then asked the following:

- How did you learn about the event?

- If you are a helper, what were you doing when you heard about the incident, and how did this affect you?

- How did you come to be there?

- What was your role?

A natural method of doing this is to go around the group and ask the questions of each person in turn—beginning with the debriefer.

Expectations and facts

Responses to the previous questions should lead into talking about the facts of the situation as each one saw, or sees, them. Thoughts and expectations should be expressed, because this gives an idea of how prepared—or ill-prepared—people were for what happened.

- Did you expect deaths and injuries?

- Did you expect to see mutilated bodies?

- Did you expect to see children suffering or dead?

- What did you expect to happen?

- What did you think at the time?

- Did you expect violence?

- How were you treated by others while you were there?

- How prepared were you for what happened?

- What did you think was happening?

Thoughts and impressions

When people in the group are describing what they saw and now see as the facts of the situation, it should lead to questions such as

- What were your first thoughts on becoming involved?

- What did you decide to do next?

- Why did you decide to do this?

Sharing impressions and facts can help group members see different perspectives on what happened and therefore see their own involvement in a different light. Some of their thoughts will be confirmed by others in the group, but they might find that their impressions, perceptions and reactions were based on incorrect information. This helps them to

- Put their own reactions into perspective

- Have a cognitive grip on the situation

- Share and integrate their own experiences

- Clarify their own and others' roles

Having a "cognitive grip" means that those involved will try to make sense of their experiences, reactions and feelings so they can come to terms with them. The purpose of this section is to bring out the thoughts that are in their minds.

Sensory impressions are also important. What did they see, touch, smell, taste, feel? Expressing sensory experiences helps people prevent or control memories that might be triggered by external stimulants at some time in the future. A picture, sound, smell or taste can cause flashbacks (or flash-forwards), and bring the past events into the present again. Talking through these helps the participants prepare to face any future experiences.

Emotional reactions

This is usually the longest part of the debriefing. Questions about expectations and facts, thoughts and impressions and sensory experiences invariably lead to answers describing feelings. "What did you *think* about . . . ?" often receives the response, "I *felt* that . . ." People will probably speak about some or all of the following, which are typical symptoms of post-trauma stress. Their presence does not mean that those who have experienced them are ill or that post-traumatic-stress disorder will develop.

- Fear
- Frustration
- Guilt
- Depression
- Shame
- Anxiety
- Regret
- Sadness
- "We are pawns in a terrible, sick game."
- Feelings of aggression
- Unreality
- Futility

- Helplessness
- Self-reproach
- Anger
- Hopelessness
- Isolation
- Bitterness
- Blame
- Failure
- Nightmares and dreams
- Intrusive thoughts
- Irritability
- Senselessness
- Conflict

Sharing feelings is important, and the leader acts as a catalyst in enabling the feelings to be expressed. Some will talk a great deal, and others will remain silent or have little to say. An effective leader will use skills to encourage all to participate as fully as they are able and will not allow a few to dominate the session. By moving around the table, the leader should be able to encourage everyone to take part.

Questions should be

- What did you feel in the beginning?

- What did you feel later?

- How did your colleagues at work treat you and what did they say?

- What about others who were with you?

- How did it feel to be separated from your own family?

- What was the worst thing you experienced?

- Did you cry and when?

- Did you swear or become angry and when?

- What happened when you went home?

- How did your wife/partner/children/family/friends react?

- What did other people ask you about the incident, how did this make you feel and what did you say to them?

Some will react in ways that they can't explain, but find disturbing.

> A man involved in a riot that lasted many days traveled home each night. One morning he woke up and thought that it had all been a bad dream. He got into his car and drove to where the incident was taking place. As he drew nearer, he realized that it was true. He turned around in the car, went home and changed the sheets on his bed.

The reactions of other people can cause problems.

> Ian, a soldier back from the Falklands War, found his
> family had arranged a celebration party. He was hailed as
> a hero, and some asked him how many Argentineans he
> had killed. He became extremely angry and refused to
> attend the party. He said later that he saw this as an
> attempt to glorify war, and he couldn't cope with it.
> Some of his friends had been killed and he had seen
> many Argentinean bodies. For Ian, there was no cause to
> celebrate. He spoke of the sheer horror and terror of the
> battlefield and contrasted this with the happy faces when
> he returned home. It made him physically sick.

In this section of the debriefing there is often a very sharp
contrast between the shattering experience of the event and the
seemingly trivial questions and answers that are given in the
group. Sometimes members of the group will recall previous
experiences that they've found distressing. If some are distressed or
cry during this stage, it is usual for others in the group to give
support. A fairly strong feeling of sharing can develop, so that
when one person is upset, others will put their arms around them
or offer verbal support. When someone is very upset, or cries, the
debriefer can ask others in the group to support them. Final
questions in this section can be

- What do you feel as you sit here?

- What are your main worries and anxieties?

The leader should take a mental note of any participants who
may need special help, but this should not be mentioned within
the group. Those who seem to need more help can be approached
privately afterward, or they may ask for further help.

Normalization

Here the leader emphasizes that the reactions and feelings
experienced are entirely normal. A brief explanation of post-trauma
stress reactions should be given to reassure people that they are
not stupid or going crazy. The debriefer can also explain the effect
this can have on their families. Dyregrov calls this stage
anticipatory guidance.

Future planning and coping

Here, the possibility of needing help and support for themselves and their families is discussed.

- What help and support do you think you need now?

- What resources are available at work and at home for you, your family and colleagues?

- How will you deal with difficult people and situations?

- Do any of your family need to talk things through?

- What about any children at home or away at school who will have heard about the incident? What help can they be given to them?

- What have you learned from others in the group?

The leader can also outline sources of help and organizations they can call on for assistance. It should, again, be stressed that these offers are confidential. Some will feel very vulnerable at this stage and might resist offers of help. They might see this as threatening them and their ability to survive.

Disengagement

This section provides an opportunity for any other questions to be raised. Further help is offered on a confidential basis as necessary. Members are also asked to discuss whether they wish to meet again in the near future, and if so, when and with whom. Some will want to meet again, but others will not wish to do so—either because they are actually coping or because they are defending themselves by the use of denial. Group members should be told that they might need help if

- The symptoms do not begin to decrease after four to six weeks, or longer in a case of personal loss or bereavement

- Symptoms increase over time

- There is a loss of function or ability at home, with the family, at work or elsewhere

- Marked personality changes occur

Participants should know where to go for help and receive a list of confidential and other telephone numbers, although some might not wish to take one.

Follow-up

There may or may not be a follow-up after the debriefing. Some debriefers see this as a necessity, while others think that it should be done only when the nature and extent of the incident and the effect on those involved requires it. If it is a "minor" incident, then a follow-up should not be necessary, and the debriefing session should be sufficient.

Keep two things in mind. First, those being debriefed must be reassured that their reactions are normal; nothing should be said or done that might suggest that they are ill, will get worse or need constant help and support. The debriefing session will help them cope and will reduce the possibility of deeper symptoms emerging later.

Second, a follow-up, if presented as the normal procedure, can help leaders evaluate reactions and confirm their progress. Participants will also know that they have support resources, should they need them. The debriefer can say that the normal procedure is that after about a month they will be contacted confidentially to confirm their progress. At this stage, some might say that they do not wish to be contacted. The debriefer should accept that this is a normal reaction to the debriefing for some people.

Summary

The leader then gives a brief summary of what has happened in the session, and can offer further help for any who might need it. The group can then disperse. Providing coffee or tea and sandwiches can provide an opportunity for less-formal discussion, although some might wish to leave immediately. Others will stay and talk. The debriefer may leave at this stage, and this can confirm the feeling that the debriefing has been accomplished and that the session is now over. Some debriefers will wish to stay and talk, but they should not ask questions about or discuss the session unless they are asked.

Conclusion

Remember that the process of psychological debriefing will help people recover who have experienced abnormal events in their lives. This kind of debriefing is not something carried out on a weekly or monthly basis. There might be a series of sessions on one day or over a few days, but they are intended as part of one continuous process. When the debriefing is over, the debriefer may not have further contact with the group members. If they wish to form a support group and meet together, they should arrange it themselves. It's important to avoid giving any impression that their reactions and present state of mind are unusual or abnormal. If this happens, they might believe that they are ill, weak or inadequate. The debriefer should feel

> My job is now over, and I have done sufficient work to help these people to cope with their feelings and emotions. They should be able to face their families, friends and colleagues with a degree of confidence now. If they have problems, they know where they can find help. I have not made them feel that they are pathetic or weak.

Debriefers will need to be debriefed themselves and talk over the session with a colleague or supervisor. They will be left with much "luggage" that they have collected from the group, and they will probably be concerned about how the group, or certain individuals in it, are coping.

The Debriefers

Those who carry out psychological debriefing must be carefully selected and trained. If not, they could do immense harm. Debriefing must not be done by those who think that they can do it without training or support. Those who are selected as debriefers must become familiar with the model and method of debriefing and must practice it through role-play. They should attend a course that consists of the following essential elements.

- Review of initial listening and counseling skills
- Explanation of post-traumatic stress reactions and its effects on individuals, families and groups
- Introduction to group dynamic principles
- Role-play, preferably with closed-circuit TV
- Discussion of any problems or questions
- Support for debriefers

General Comments

Psychological debriefing is an essential part of the process in helping people to cope with the aftereffects of post-trauma stress and to prevent the development of post-traumatic stress disorder. It should include all those people who have been involved in a traumatic incident, including victims, survivors, carers and helpers. The method and model evolved by Atle Dyregrov and J.T. Mitchell can successfully be adapted for use with people after

- Accidents
- Robberies
- Disasters
- Divorce and separation
- Shootings
- Bombings
- Hostage situations
- Rape, war and combat, and other acts of violence

It can also be used after particularly distressing events involving bereavement and loss, such as suicides, murder and multiple deaths and also lengthy, unsuccessful rescue attempts. Those in authority should ensure that psychological debriefing is not viewed as an option or an "extra," but is included as a normal part of the response to accidents and disaster. It should be standard operating procedure among these professions.

I would like to see a nationally organized and funded body to dispatch debriefing teams to accidents, disasters and other traumatic events. These teams can be called upon when needed to give advice and help to those on the scene. This team should be multidisciplinary and the personnel selected and trained specifically for this kind of situation.

Following a hostage situation that occurred before the Gulf War, a team of debriefers consisting of clergy, social workers and hospital social service personnel was formed. All had considerable counseling experience. Some felt unable to use the psychological debriefing model and chose to act in a supporting role, either within the debriefing groups or outside, with children and other family members. They were also able to help those who chose to leave the groups during the sessions. This team was supported and assisted by a leader, two psychiatrists and a clinical psychologist, all of whom were experienced in the process of psychological debriefing.

Such a group of debriefers could be organized and trained nationally or locally and be made available when there are traumatic incidents. Many organizations could have their own counselors trained in psychological debriefing or should be able to call upon professional debriefers or consultants from outside. There should also be a process of education for all carers and helpers and those in positions of leadership and authority.

Implementation could be done nationally with the help of local authorities (health, education and social service departments), the armed forces, the police, fire and rescue and other state, provincial, county and city services. Voluntary organizations could also be involved. All these organizations, especially those involved in counseling, can include awareness training on post-trauma stress reactions as part of the overall program. Some counselors could be trained as debriefers. Victims and helpers who suffer the effects of trauma, whatever the cause, will need to be supported, to the greatest extent possible, during and following the event. While the incident is taking place, this support is known as *defusing,* and consists of the usual and familiar responses. These include

- Being aware of the coping mechanisms that are being exhibited
- Giving verbal and physical support
- Allowing rest periods
- Providing medical attention and counseling support

Once the incident is over, the "defusing" should continue. For helpers and carers this normally consists of

- A debriefing meeting with those in charge when immediate experiences and practical problems can be discussed
- Medical examinations if necessary
- Brief counseling support
- A period of rest and a return to work

This defusing stage depends on the nature of the event and whether it is for a victim or helper.

> Some bank personnel were involved in an armed robbery. After the incident was over, they were sent for a medical checkup and given some time off. The area manager called to see them and they received letters of support and bouquets of flowers. Counseling was made available, but all declined the offer.
>
> The victim of a traffic accident was taken to the hospital, where she was given excellent medical attention and lots of "tender loving care" by the nursing staff. The nurses, doctors and the chaplain gave her reassurance, and her family visited regularly, bringing the inevitable fruit baskets and flowers. On leaving the hospital a few days later, she was allowed a few days rest and then returned to work.

Defusing like this is excellent and necessary and is normal practice for most occasions, but is not sufficient after a trauma. Psychological debriefing, carried out by trained personnel two days or so after the event, and in some cases much later, enables victims or helpers to talk through the incident in an informal but structured way. It provides a forum for them to talk about their impressions, reactions and feelings and, through sharing with the group, helps them make some kind of sense of what they have experienced. It will reduce tensions and feelings of abnormality and encourages them to mobilize and utilize their own resources and those of the group or organization to which they belong.

Psychological debriefing will also prepare them for any future reactions. Above all, it reassures them that they are normal people reacting in normal ways to an abnormal experience. Spouses or partners can also be included in the debriefings. If not, they should certainly be made aware of the nature of the incident and the possible effects upon them and the relationship. The effects on any children in the families also need to be considered.

By having help and support like this available through psychological debriefing, those who experience traumatic events can be helped to continue more successfully with their lives. This is not an optional extra or luxury for a few. Neither is it only for those who appear to suffer or for those who request it. It is a necessary and essential element of any response to those who experience trauma of any kind.

Without psychological debriefing, some will suffer unnecessarily and a few will experience long-term problems, even months or years later. The benefits for individuals, families, groups and society in general are inestimable. I'll let Atle Dyregrov have the last word:

> By providing survivors, bereaved and helpers in disasters with rapid help, and by building on the internal strengths of the affected groups, we may prevent much of the unnecessary pain and agony experienced by these groups.

I certainly hope that we can prevent post-traumatic-stress reactions in the future, not only by psychological debriefings, but by building a better system for crisis situation intervention. Debriefings, in addition to other measures, can accelerate normal recovery and prevent post-traumatic stress disorder.

The Psychological Debriefing Process

Introduction

Introduce self and explain the rules

You don't need to speak.

Confidentiality inside and outside the group.

Emphasis is on the here and now.

Explain that they might feel worse to begin with but this is normal.

The debrief is not a forum for complaints.

Expectations and facts

What did you expect would happen?

What did happen?

What did you see and experience?

What were your thoughts at the time?

Did you expect violence, dead bodies and carnage?

How were you treated by others?

Thoughts and impressions

What were your first thoughts?

What did you decide to do and why?

What were your impressions then and now?

What did you see, hear, smell, touch, taste?

Emotional reactions

Thoughts lead to feelings.

What was the worst about what happened?

What were your reactions at the time and later?

What were your physical reactions?

What did you make of what you saw and experienced?

Normalization

Comment on reactions—they are normal.

Give anticipatory guidelines—explain what might be felt and what reactions can occur.

Future planning and coping

Mobilize support.

Ask what resources they have available at work and home.

Who can help and what help do they need?

Give advice on coping and on those who can help.

What about family, children and work?

Disengagement

Any questions?

Explain possible development of symptoms.

Symptoms should decrease in near future.

If symptoms persist for four weeks or more, attendees might need professional help.

Look for any loss of function or changes in ability at home, work or elsewhere.

Give a summary of what has happened in the debriefing.

Do they want follow-up meetings? When and where?

Summary

The debriefer gives a brief summary of the session. Let the group disperse, but check any who might show particular symptoms of distress. These might be the result of the debriefing or of deeper stress—or both.

Notes for Debriefers

The debriefer should prepare a list of questions related to the situation and incident. The following open list gives general headings, under which appropriate notes or questions can be listed.

Check list for debriefers

Introduction

Introduce self. Explain debriefing and explain rules.
How did you learn about the event?
What happened before it took place?
Where were you?

Expectations and facts

What did you expect to happen?
What happened?

Thoughts

What were your thoughts?
What did you do and why?

Impressions

What were/are your main impressions and memories?
What did you see hear, smell, touch, taste?

Emotions

How did you feel at the time?
What made you most upset?
Did you cry?

Reactions

How do you feel now?

Leaving

What happened when you went home?
How did spouse and family react?

What did others say that was helpful/unhelpful?

Normalization

Explain normality of reactions to post-trauma stress.

The future

What help do you and your family need now?
What resources are available at work/home/elsewhere?
Thank people for coming and taking part.

Prepare the questions under each section above beforehand and base them on knowledge of what has happened. The questions must be appropriate, accurate and related to the particular incident and people involved. The questions asked in some cases will be very different from those asked in others.

For example, if you know you are to debrief after a car crash in which people were killed, you will need to prepare questions that are different from those following an accident where no one was killed. Also, the involvement of children and the deaths of children raises the possible level of response and reaction.

Examples
1. A car accident with deaths
Expectations and facts

Did you expect to see dead bodies?
How did you react to the bodies?
Where did you find them and what did they look like?
Did you expect the car to burst into flames?

Did you try to rescue anybody? Why? Why not?

Thoughts

What did you think when you saw the bodies?

What do you think now?

What did you think about most?

Impressions

What were your main impressions of the bodies and injured?

What smells? Burned flesh, gasoline, diesel?

What sights? Charred bodies? Clothing, and so on?

What sounds? Screaming, shouting, moaning?

What touch? Bodies, metal, glass?

2. A violent bank robbery

Expectations and facts

What did the robber look like when you first saw him?

At first, what did you believe he wanted?

When did you realize that it was a robbery?

When did you first see the gun/weapon?

Thoughts

What did you think when you saw he was wearing a hood/ mask/carrying a gun?

What did you think about being threatened?

Impressions

What smells? Body sweat, fear, gun powder, gun-oil?

What sights? Weapons, violence, robber's eyes/mouth?

What sounds? Shooting, shouting, screaming, threats?

What touch? By the gun? Were you hit/abused physically?

Emotions

Did you feel helpless, angry, afraid, violent, degraded?

Did you think you might be killed? When?

What did you feel about others involved? Women?

How do you feel now as a man/the bank manager?

Make the questions relevant to each unique situation. If a child, spouse, relative or friend is involved, the questions should be thought out very sensitively.

3. An accident with the deaths of children

Expectations and facts

Did you expect to see a dead child/children?

What did you do when you found the body?

What did it look like?

Thoughts

What did you think when you saw the little body?

What do you think might have been different if it had been an adult?

Did you feel anger, sorrow, horror, injustice?

Impressions

What were your impressions of the scene that involved a dead child?

What smells? Diapers, talcum, blood?

What sights? The little body, injuries, blood, toys?

What sounds? Crying, parents upset?

What touch? The body, clothing, toys?

Emotions

Did you cry? When and why?

What upset you most?

What were the reactions of others?
  Police, rescuers, parents, friends, colleagues?

The questions would be different for a suicide, murder, minor accident, national disaster, shooting, hostage situation or a war, if the incident was sudden and unexpected or if people had time to experience fear and terror for some time before the incident took place. The questions also depend on who was being debriefed. Men may be more defensive in answering questions about feelings than women or if other men are present. They may respond in a different manner if they are with close friends, family or colleagues.

Professional helpers or survivors who are being debriefed might ask other questions and have other concerns, especially about being involved and perhaps not being able to help:

Doctors. Their ability or inability to save life.

Clergy. Questions about meaning, purpose and faith.

Single people. Questions about the value of getting married or having children or seeing dead children.

Police. Questions about blame and responsibility.

Parents. When their own children are killed—questions about injustice and their responsibility and possible failure as parents. *Survivors and helpers*—identification with their own children. It might happen to them.

Helpers. Fire and rescue workers, nurses, ambulance personnel and many others might feel especially helpless and useless and express frustration, anger and rage.

The debriefing session should ensure that the model is adhered to and worked through, and that the questions are asked in a sensitive manner, but don't let those being debriefed avoid the point of the questions.

Typical Effects of Post-Trauma Stress on Relationships

There may be changes in the way people see themselves, their wife, husband, partner or children. Relationships can become strained and difficult, with communication problems.

Communication problems. If one person is suffering, he or she might not be able to talk to his or her partner and may retreat behind a wall of silence or suppressed anger.

Inability to stop talking about the event. This can become irritating and boring for others whose response might be to tell them to shut up and forget about it.

Nightmares and dreams. Waking up in a panic or sweats. This can be very disturbing and frightening for partners also. Suddenly jumping out of bed.

Feeling that life is a waste of time. "What's the point?" Apathy. Partners can become angry about this.

Inability to make even simple decisions. Loss of concentration. Disinterest in families, friends, hobbies. Others can wonder what this is about and become frustrated and angry.

Feelings of vulnerability. Anxiety about the same things happening again. Confusion and disorientation. The response can be to tell the person to pull himself together.

Pent-up feelings can result in anger and violence in the relationship, sometimes without any apparent cause. Shouting and pleading against anything or nothing.

Loss of self-esteem or self-value and worth. "I am useless. Why bother?" Partners can respond by arguing or trying to convince the spouse that this is not true and stress the value of their relationship, the family and home.

Loss of interest in work or hobbies. Changing jobs. Wanting to move to another home. All cause upheaval in the family and seem so unnecessary to others.

Looking for new relationships or partners. Dissatisfaction with present partner or family.

Constant preoccupation with the incident. Keeping a diary of events or a scrapbook. This can infuriate others.

Avoiding anything to do with the incident. Keeping away from people, including those who are there to help.

A lack of understanding on the part of the person experiencing the incident of the effects that the trauma or their behavior has on others in the family.

Shame and fear about behavior, especially of guilt or lack of ability to cope at the time and subsequently. "I should have done this, and I shouldn't be like this."

Feeling like a complete failure. "I did not do what I could or should have done. I did not behave like a man. I am even lower than an animal. I feel utterly degraded."

The Stockholm Syndrome

During a raid on a bank in Stockholm years ago, some people were held hostage by the robbers. Certain characteristics of the behavior of both captors and captives were noticed then and have been noticed in similar hostage-taking incidents since then. These symptoms are known as *the Stockholm syndrome*. Basically, hostages develop feelings of sympathy and empathy with those who are holding them.

Also, the captors develop sympathy with their prisoners. The characteristics are

Blame

Those who are held hostage direct their anger and frustration at those in authority. They must have someone to blame—similar to certain reactions in bereavement. They might even blame others in the group of hostages.

Sympathy and empathy

Captives can come to believe that those who are holding them are not as bad as they first thought. They begin to see them as real human beings. Every little kindness shown to them is thought of as a sign that the captors must really be decent people. In a long-term hostage situation, the release of one hostage is hailed with joy, and there is sometimes the feeling, "Well, they can't be all that bad, can they? They have set someone free."

For the syndrome to develop, it doesn't seem to matter that the captives were held for days, months or years. Similarly, the captors can develop close feelings and attachments to the hostages. In some cases, hostages have joined

captors. It is likely that in many hostage situations the captors will distance themselves from the hostages to prevent such closeness from developing.

It may be more difficult to cope with hostages when such a relationship has developed. Conversely, it might be advantageous to their cause for the captors to encourage such a relationship, especially if the captives begin to speak highly of them and criticize their own authorities. The political as well as personal implications of this are important.

Hostage-taking can be a powerful method of influencing individuals, groups or nations. A number of people who were held hostage overseas said on their return that those who held them treated them well, and they felt sympathy for their captors' cause. While they had lost everything they possessed, many of them still seemed unable to hate their captors for what they had done. Much of their anger was turned against their own country's authorities at all levels, both at home and in the country where they were held.

This anger was still in evidence, and in some cases had deepened, two years later. This is typical of the Stockholm syndrome. Those who may be held hostage should be aware that such a relationship might develop. It can affect the relationships between those held hostage and their captors. On their return to freedom, it can continue to influence the way they think and feel about themselves, their fellow hostages and their captors. It will also affect relationships with their families and friends and in some measure determine how they survive and cope.

Further Reading and Useful Addresses

Further Reading

Note: Some of these books may be out of print, but they should still be available through libraries.

General Readings

Colodzin, Benjamin. *How to Survive Trauma: A Program for War Veterans & Survivors of Rape, Assault, Abuse or Environmental Disasters.* Revised ed. Barrytown, NY: Barrytown Ltd., 1997.

Flannery, Jr., Raymond B. *Post-Traumatic Stress Disorder: The Victim's Guide to Healing & Recovery.* New York: Crossroad Publishing Company, 1995.

Herman, Judith L. *Trauma & Recovery: The Aftermath of Violence from Domestic Abuse to Political Terror.* New York: Basic Books, 1997.

Levine, Howard. *Prisoners of the Past: overcoming Post-Traumatic Stress Disorder.* The PIA Press, 1992.

Matsakis, Aphrodite. *I Can't Get Over It: A Handbook for Trauma Survivors.* New York: New Harbinger Publications, 1996.

Skynner, Robin, and John Cleese. *Families & How to Survive Them.* New York and London: Oxford University Press, Inc., 1984.

Professional Reading

American Psychiatric Association Staff. *Diagnostic & Statistical Manual of Mental Disorders.* 4th ed. American Psychiatric Press, Inc., 1995.

Bisbey, Stephen, and Lori Beth Bisby. *Brief Therapy for Post-Traumatic Stress Disorder: Traumatic Incident Reduction and Related Techniques.* New York: John Wiley & Sons, 1998.

Brown, Sandra L. *Counseling Victims of Violence.* American Counseling Association, 1991.

Davidson, Jonathan R.; Edna B. Foa, eds. *Post-Traumatic Stress Disorder: DSM-1V & Beyond.* Washington, D.C.: American Psychiatric Press, Inc., 1992.

Everstine, Diane S.; Louis Everstine. *The Trauma Response: Treatment for Emotional Injury.* New York: W.W. Norton & Company, 1993.

Figley, Charles R. *Compassion Fatigue: Coping with Secondary Traumatic Stress Disorder in Those Who Treat the Traumatized.* Levittown, PA: Brunner/Mazel Pub., 1995.

Figley, Charles R., ed. *Trauma & Its Wake, Vol. 1: The Study & Treatment of Post-Traumatic Stress Disorder.* Levittown, PA: Brunner/Mazel Publishers, 1985.

—*Trauma & Its Wake, Vol. 2: Traumatic Stress Theory, Research, & Intervention.* Levittown, PA: Brunner/Mazel Publishers, 1986.

Foy, David W., ed. *Treating PTSD: Cognitive-Behavioral Strategies.* New York: Guilford Press, 1992.

Giller, Earl, ed. *Biological Assessment & Treatment of Post-Traumatic Stress Disorder.* Washington, D.C.: American Psychiatric Press, Inc., 1990.

Kasnevitch, Peter J. *Stress Disorders in Post-Traumatic Conditions.* Washington, D.C.: ABBE Publishers Association, 1988.

Kluft, Richard P., ed. *Incest-Related Syndromes of Adult Psychopathology.* Washington, D.C.: American Psychiatric Press, Inc., 1990.

McCann, I. Lisa; Laurie A. Pearlman. *Psychological Trauma & the Adult Survivor: Theory, Therapy, & Transformation.* Levittown, PA: Brunner/Maze Publishers, 1990.

Ochberg, Frank M. *Post-Traumatic Therapy & Victims of Violence.* Levittown, PA: Brunner/Mazel Publishers, 1988.

Saigh, Philip A., ed. *Post-Traumatic Stress Disorder: A Comprehensive Test.* Allyn & Bacon, Inc., 1999.

Scott, Michael J., and Stephen G. Stradling. *Counseling for Post-Traumatic Stress Disorder.* Newbury Park, CA: Sage Publications, Inc., 1992.

Ulman, Richard B., and Doris Brothers. *The Shattered Self: Psychoanalytic Study of Trauma*. Hillsdale, NJ: Analytic Press, 1988.

Van der Kolk, Bessel A. *Psychological Trauma*. Washington, D.C.: American Psychiatric Press, Inc., 1987.

Waites, Elizabeth A. *Memory Quest: Trauma and the Search for Personal History*. New York: W.W. Norton & Company, Inc., 1997.

Wilson, John P. *Trauma, Transformation, & Healing: An Integrative Approach to Theory, Research, & Post Traumatic Therapy*. Levittown, PA: Brunner/Mazel Publishers, 1989.

Wilson, J. P., and B. Raphael, eds. *International Handbook of Traumatic Stress Syndromes*. New York: Plenum Publishing Corporation, 1993.

Wolf, Marion, and Aron Mosnaim, eds. *Post-Traumatic Stress Disorder Etiology, Phenomenology, & Treatment*. Washington, D.C.: American Psychiatric Press, Inc., 1990.

Catastrophes/Disasters

Austin, Linda S., ed. *Responding to Disaster: A Guide for Mental Health Professionals*. Washington, D.C.: American Psychiatric Press, Inc., 1992.

Gist, Richard. *Psychosocial Aspects of Disaster*. New York: John Wiley & Sons, Inc., 1989.

HMSO Staff. *Disasters: Planning for a Caring Response*. New York: UNIPUB, 1991.

Hodgkinson, Peter, and Michael Stewart. *Coping with Catastrophe: A Handbook of Disaster Management*. New York: Routledge, 1991.

National Institute of Mental Health Staff; Barbara J. Sowder and Mary Lystad, eds. *Disasters & Mental Health: Contemporary Perspectives & Innovation in Services to Disaster Victims*. Washington, D.C.: American Psychiatric Press, Inc., 1986.

Raphael, Beverley. *When Disaster Strikes: How Communities & Individuals Cope with Catastrophe*. New York: Basic Books, 1986.

Ursano, Robert J., Brian G. McCaughey, and Carol S. Fullerton. *Individual & Community Responses to Trauma & Disaster: The Structure of Human Chaos*. New York: Cambridge University Press, 1996.

Coping

Beattie, Melody. *Codependent No More: How to Stop Controlling Others & Start Caring for Yourself*. 2nd ed. Center City, MN: Hazelden Foundation, 1987.

Bettelheim, Bruno. *The Informed Heart: Autonomy in a Mass Age*. New York: Free Press, 1960.

Bradshaw, John. *Healing the Shame that Binds You*. Deerfield Beach, FL: Health Communications, Inc., 1988.

Deits, Bob. *Life after Loss: A Personal Guide to Dealing with Death, Divorce, Job Change & Relocation*, Third Edition. Tucson, AZ: Fisher Books, 2000.

Flannery, Jr., Raymond B. *Becoming Stress-Resistant through the Project SMART Program*. New York: Crossroad Publishing Company, 1993.

Lazarus, Richard S.; Susan Folkman. *Stress, Appraisal, & Coping*. New York: Springer Publishing Company, Inc., 1984.

Lewis, C. S. *A Grief Observed*. San Francisco, CA: HarperSanFrancisco, 1995.

Peck, M. Scott. *People of the Lie: The Hope for Healing Human Evil*. New York: Simon & Schuster, 1997.

Pennebaker, James W. *Opening Up: The Healing Power of Expressing Emotions*. New York: Guilford Press, 1997.

Selye, Hans. *The Stress of Life*. New York: McGraw-Hill, Inc., 1978.

Worden, J. William. *Grief Counseling & Grief Therapy: A Handbook for the Mental Health Practitioner*. 2nd ed. New York: Springer Publishing Company, Inc., 1991.

Children

Eth, Spencer, and Robert S. Pynoos. *Post-Traumatic Stress Disorder in Children*. Washington, D.C.: American Psychiatric Press, Inc., 1985.

Goodwin, Jean M., ed. *Rediscovering Childhood Trauma: Historical Casebook and Clinical Applications*. Washington, D.C.: American Psychiatric Press, Inc., 1993.

Palmer, Pat. *Good Grief*. San Luis Obispo, CA: Impact Publishers, 1994.

Saylor, C. F., ed. *Children and Disasters*. New York: Plenum Publishing Corporation, 1993.

Multiple-Personality Disorders

Cohen, Barry M.; Esther Giller, eds. *Multiple Personality Disorder from the Inside Out*. Lutherville, Md.: Sidran Press, 1991.

Putnam, Frank W. *Diagnosis and Treatment of Multiple Personality Disorder*. New York: Guilford Press, 1989.

Sexual Abuse

Bass, Ellen; Laura Davis. *The Courage to Heal: A Guide for Women Survivors of Child Sexual Abuse*. New York: Harper Perennial Library, 1994.

Blume, E. Sue. *Secret Survivors: Uncovering Incest & Its Aftereffects in Women*. New York: Ballantine Books, Inc., 1998.

Brownmiller, Susan. *Against Our Will: Men, Women and Rape*. New York: Fawcett Book Group, 1993.

Butler, Sandra. *Conspiracy of Silence: The Trauma of Incest*. Updated ed. Volcano, CA: Volcano Press, Inc., 1996.

Kritsberg, Wayne. *The Invisible Wound: Healing Childhood Sexual Abuse*. New York: Bantam Books, Inc., 1993.

Lew, Mike. *Victims No Longer: Men Recovering form Incest and Other Childhood Sexual Abuse*. New York: HarperCollins Publishers, Inc., 1990.

Maltz, Wendy. *The Sexual Healing Journey: A Guide for Survivors of Sexual Abuse*. New York: HarperCollins Publishers, Inc., 1992.

Warshaw, Robin. *I Never Called It Rape: The Ms. Report on Recognizing, Fighting, and Surviving Date Rape*. New York: HarperCollins Publishers, Inc., 1994.

Torture/War Refugees/Holocaust Victims

Basoglu, Metin., ed. *Torture and Its Consequences: Current Treatment Approaches*. New York: Cambridge University Press, 1998.

Davidson, Shamai Charny. *Holding on to Humanity—The Message of Holocast Survivors: The Shamai Davidson Papers*. New York: New York University Press, 1992.

Randall, Glenn R., and Ellen L. Lutz. *Serving Survivors of Torture*. Washington, D.C.: American Association for the Advancement of Science, 1991.

Van der Veer, Guus. *Counseling and Therapy with Refugees: Psychological Problems of Victims of War, Torture and Repression*. John Wiley & Sons, Inc., 1992.

Vietnam Veterans

Dean, Chuck. *Nam Vet: Making Peace with Your Past*. Revised and expanded ed. Questar Publishers, Inc., 1990.

Dicks, Shirley. *From Vietnam to Hell: Interviews with Victims of Post-Traumatic Stress Disorder*. Jefferson, NC: McFarland & Company, Inc., Publishers, 1990.

Hansel, Sarah, Ann Steidle, Grace Zaczek and Ron Zaczek. *Soldier's Heart: Survivors' Views of Combat Trauma*. Lutherville, MD: Sidran Press, 1994.

Kelly, William E., ed. *Post-Traumatic Stress Disorder and the War Veteran*. Levittown, PA: Brunner/Mazel Publishers, 1985.

Kuenning, Delores A. *Life after Vietnam: How Veterans & Their Loved Ones Can Heal the Psychological Wounds of War*. New York: Paragon House Publishers, 1991.

Levin, Barry, David O. Ferrier and Susan Caney-Peterson, eds. *Defending the Vietnam Combat Veteran*. Vietnam Veterans Legal Assistance Project, 1989.

Mason, Patience. *Recovering from the War: A Woman's Guide to Helping Your Vietnam Veteran, Your Family and Yourself*. New York: Penguin Books, 1990.

Preston, John. *Growing Beyond Emotional Pain: Action Plans for Healing*. San Luis Obispo, CA: Impact Publishers, 1993.

Sonnenberg, Stephen M., Arthur S. Blank and John A. Talbott, eds. *The Trauma of War, Stress and Recovery in Vietnam Veterans,* Washington, D.C.: American Psychiatric Press, 1985.

Useful Addresses— United States

International Society for Traumatic Stress Studies
60 Revere Drive, Ste. 500
Northbrook, IL 60062
(847) 480-9028
(847) 480-9282 (fax)
http://www.istss.org

National Center for Post-Traumatic Stress Disorder
VAM & ROC 116-D
Rural Route 5
White River Junction, VT 05009
(802) 296-5132
ptsd@dartmouth.edu
http://www.ncptsd.org

National Institute of Mental Health
Anxiety Disorders Education Program
5600 Fishers Lane
Rockville, MD 20857
(301) 443-2403
http://www.nimh.nih.gov/anxiety/anxiety/ptsd/index.htm

National Organization for Victim Assistance
1757 Park Rd., NW
Washington, D.C. 20010
(202) 232-6682

National Victim Center
2111 Wilson Blvd., Ste. 300
Arlington, VA 22201
(703) 276-2880
(703) 276-2889 (fax)
http://www.nvc.org

Post-Trauma Resources
1830 Bull St.
Columbia, SC 29201
(803) 765-0700
(803) 765-1607 (fax)
info@posttrauma.com
http://www.postrauma.com/ptsvc.html

Sidran Foundation
2328 W. Joppa Rd., Ste. 15
Lutherville, MD 21093
(410) 825-8888
sidran@sidran.og
http://www.sidran.org

Recovery, Inc.
802 N. Dearborn St.
Chicago, IL 60610
(312) 337-5661
http://www.recovery-inc.com

Borderline Personality Disorders
http: www.BPDCentral.com
Support resources for family of persons with borderline
personality disorder.

Vietnam Veterans
Disabled American Veterans
National Headquarters
3725 Alexandria Pike
Cold Spring, KY 41076
(606) 441-7300
feedback@davmail.org
http://www.dav.org

National Center for PTSD
VA Medical Center (116D)
White River Junction, VT 05001
(802) 296-5132
(802) 296-5135 (fax)
email: ptsd@dartmouth.edu
http://www.ncptsd.org
A research and education program of
the U.S. Department of Veterans Affairs

**U.S. Veterans Affairs Mental Health
and Behavioral Sciences Services**
#915 (116)
810 Vermont Ave., N.W.
Washington, DC 20410
(202) 273-8446
http://www.va.gov

**U.S. Veterans Affairs Readjustment
Counseling Service (10B/RC)**
810 Vermont Ave., N.W.
Washington, DC 20410
(202) 273-8964
http://www.va.gov

Useful Addresses—
Canada
Canadian Mental Health Associates
National Office
2160 Yonge St., Third Floor
Toronto, Ontario M4S 2Z3
(416) 484-7750
Toronto metropolitan area office:
    (416) 789-7957

Initiative **(National Newsletter)**
Canadian Council on Social
Development
P.O. Box 3505, Station C
Ottawa, Ontario K1Y 4G1

**Ontario Association of Distress
Centers**
99 Atlantic Rd.
Toronto, Ontario M6K 3J8
(416) 537-7373

**Self-Help Clearinghouse of
Metropolitan Toronto**
40 Orchard View Blvd.
Toronto, Ontario M4R 1B9
(416) 487-4355

**Canadian Center for Victims of
Torture**
194 Gervis St., second floor
Toronto, Ontario M5B 2B7
(416) 363-1066
http://www.icomm.ca/ccvt

Computer Database
and Web Sites
PILOTS
http://www.ncptsd.org/PILOTS.
    html
        PILOTS is a bibliographic
database covering published
international literature on traumatic
stress. It is produced at the
headquarters of the National Center for
Post-Traumatic Stress Disorder (see
listing above).
        Its goal is to include citations to
all literature on post-traumatic stress
disorder, without disciplinary, linguistic,
or geographical limitations, and to offer
both current and retrospective
coverage. The web master of the site is
Fred Lerner, D.L.S.
Information Scientist
National Center for Post-Traumatic
    Stress Disorder (116D)
VA Medical Center
White River Junction, VT 05009

Critical Incident Stress site
http://www.geocities.com/
    CapitolHill/Lobby/3082
For emergency services personnel.

**David Baldwin's Trauma
Information Pages**
http://www.trauma-
pages.com/index.phtml

**Police Officers and Post-traumatic
Stress Disorder**
http://pw1.netcom.com/~jpmock/
    ptsd.htm

Site for web-page links about stress:
http://imt.net/~randolfi/StressLinks/
    html

V.O.I.C.E.S. in Action
http://www.voices-action.org/
A web site dedicated to helping victims
of incest.